Be Still and
Get Going

Also by Alan Lew

8 Monologs (poems), 1980

One God Clapping:
The Spiritual Path of a Zen Rabbi
(with Sherril Jaffe), 1999

This Is Real and You
Are Completely Unprepared:
The Days of Awe as a Journey
of Transformation, 2003

Be Still and Get Going

A Jewish Meditation Practice for Real Life

Alan Lew

Little, Brown and Company
New York • Boston

Little, Brown and Company
Time Warner Book Group
1271 Avenue of the Americas, New York, NY 10020
Visit our Web site at www.twbookmark.com

First Edition: August 2005

Library of Congress Cataloging-in-Publication Data

Lew, Alan.
    Be still and get going : A Jewish meditation practice for real life / Alan Lew. — 1st ed.
        p.   cm.
      ISBN 0-316-73910-3
      1. Meditation — Judaism.   2. Spiritual life — Judaism.   3. Bible.
O. T. Pentateuch — Criticism, interpretation, etc.   I. Title.

BM723.L52   2005
296.7'2 — DC22   2004020124

10 9 8 7 6 5 4 3 2

Q-FF

Book Design by Meryl Sussman Levavi

Printed in the United States of America

For Zoketsu Norman Fischer

Ancient Friend, Fellow Traveler

But Moses said to the people, "Don't be afraid. Collect yourselves and see the salvation which Adonai will make for you today. . . . Adonai will fight for you and you will be still." Then Adonai said to Moses, "Why do you cry out to me? Tell the Israelites to just get going."

—Exodus 14:13–15

Contents

Be Still and
Get Going

The Treasure in the Oven

SOMETIMES WE CAN LEARN MORE FROM THE MISREADING of a story than we can from the story itself. So it is with the oft-told Yiddish tale about Azyk, the son of Reb Yekl of Cracow. Azyk dreamed one night that he saw a great treasure hidden under the Praga side of the Warsaw bridge. So he woke up early the next morning and went to Warsaw. When he got to the bridge, he wanted to go to the spot where he had dreamed the treasure was hidden, but there was a watchman standing guard there. Azyk paced back and forth on the bridge all day long and into the night, but the watchman never budged. In fact he finally became aware of Azyk and his pacing, so he approached him and asked him what he was doing there. Azyk told him the truth. He had come to the Warsaw bridge because he had dreamed the night before that a treasure was hidden there. That's funny, the watchman said, I dreamed of a great treasure last night too, only this one was hidden in the oven of a house belonging to a man named Azyk, the son of Reb Yekl of Cracow. Astonished, Azyk turned right around and went home, and sure enough, when he opened his oven door, he found a great treasure there and became a very rich man.

It's true, of course, as this story suggests, that we often look far afield for the things we value most, when they are usually found close to home, but this story makes a number of other important points as well. Azyk has the courage to follow his dream, and the wisdom not to give up on it even when it seems to have carried him in the wrong direction. And he is open enough to learn from the dream of another, even when it comes from a different people and a different religious tradition, in this case the non-Jewish watchman.

But in recent years this story has been told — and more important, mistold — to make a very particular point. In all the versions of this story I have heard over the last twenty years, the treasure was hidden not in Azyk's oven, but rather beneath his house, and these versions of the story usually end with Azyk's digging up the buried treasure. There is a reason for this recasting of the story; it is usually told as an object lesson for the many Jews who have turned to other religions — to Buddhism, to Hinduism, and others — for spiritual gratification. The story is invoked to say to them, Look, you have a great treasure buried beneath your own house. You've followed your dream of spiritual riches far and wide — all the way to the Warsaw bridge — but the treasure has been hidden beneath your own house all this time. Why travel elsewhere? Why travel far and wide, when all you have to do is dig up the treasure that has been beneath your own house all the while?

Why the change in the ending of the story? I am convinced that it is because in this analogy the treasure buried beneath the house represents Kabala, the esoteric, mystical branch of Judaism, and the secret or buried teachings, the ones that have to be dug up. The people who tell this version of the story are saying, in effect, You don't need Buddhism, you don't need Yoga, you don't need meditation; you have Kabala, a treasure buried right in your own backyard!

But in the original version of the story, the treasure is not buried beneath the house. It is not a secret. It is hidden in the oven, in the kitchen, in the most frequently used room in the house. It is hidden in plain sight. It doesn't need to be dug up at all. All one has to do is go to the most obvious, least exotic place in the house and simply open the door. In my opinion this story reflects our spiritual reality much more precisely than the altered version.

There is an open secret embedded in the sacred literature of Judaism. This literature — the Torah, the Hebrew Bible, the Talmud, Midrash, Kabala, and the Teachings of the Hasidic Masters — is generally read as the wellspring of Jewish communal values and religious observance. But there is a much deeper and more universal message sitting right in plain view, on the surface of these texts — a message largely unseen for the three thousand years of their existence. If one knows what to look for, the classical sources of Judaism offer a trenchant guide to spiritual practice. The striking thing is that we find this guidebook not only in the esoteric teachings of Judaism, where we might expect to find them, but also right in front of our faces in some of Judaism's most familiar material — in the well-known stories and teachings of the Torah and the Talmud. In other words, we find these teachings not buried beneath the house, but right in the middle of it, right in the kitchen, in the most obvious place of all, where anyone could find them.

At Makor Or, the meditation center I established in San Francisco at the turn of the millennium with my dear friend Norman Fischer, we have emphasized the considerable spiritual power of traditional, normative Jewish practice — prayer, Torah study, and a deep immersion in the Sabbath — and the equally impressive capacity of mindfulness meditation to open us to this power. The practice we have developed at Makor Or is not based on dubious re-creations of Kabalistic meditation practices that may or may not have ever existed, but rather on the rock-solid certainty of two intact traditions — mindfulness meditation and normative Judaism.

Most contemporary experiments in Jewish meditation or spirituality have relied heavily on Kabala. At Makor Or we have tended to shy away from Kabala for a number of reasons. First of all, almost all the Kabalistic texts that we have in our possession speak primarily about the fruits of Kabala. They describe the mystical states to which Kabala transports us in vivid detail, but for the most part the journey itself is missing. The nuts and bolts of Kabalistic practice are never found in these texts. These practices were rarely reduced to writing; rather they were handed down person to person by an unbroken chain of teachers. One of the overlooked consequences of the Holocaust is that this chain was largely broken. Most of the major teachers of Kabala still lived in

Europe at the time of the Holocaust, and in far too many cases the techniques and practices they bore in their person perished when they did.

Contemporary teachers of Kabala have often engaged in speculative attempts to reinvent Kabalistic practices, or to give Kabalistic subtitles to meditative practices they learned elsewhere, particularly from Tibetan and Vipassana Buddhism. It has become increasingly clear over the past several decades that what is really essential in spiritual work is the daily, disciplined practice of spirituality — not the highs we might experience at a weekend retreat or a workshop or a hike at Yosemite, but the essential work of connecting ourselves to the transcendent every day of our lives.

What we have found at Makor Or is that we don't need to get fancy or exotic about spiritual practice. The particular moment of Jewish spiritual practice — prayer, study, and the observance of Shabbat — is sufficiently charged on its own. When we are opened to this moment by mindfulness meditation, we begin to see its full richness. And wherever we look in the normative tradition of Jewish sacred literature, we begin to see references to mindfulness practice. In fact we begin to see that right there in plain sight is a guide to an entire spiritual practice, a path that carries us inexorably toward ourselves and our mission in life.

I was a serious practitioner of Zen meditation for ten years. Then I became a Conservative rabbi and a seriously observant Jew for another fifteen years after that. Norman Fischer is a Zen master and the former abbot of the San Francisco Zen Center, and has been a devoted Jew all his life. As a boy he attended minyan every day and studied Talmud with his rabbi, with whom he has sustained an important spiritual connection. For the past ten years, first at workshops and retreats and then finally in our own meditation center, we have been practicing mindfulness meditation side by side with ordinary Jewish spiritual activities. The members of our formal practice period meditate together early in the morning and then go next door to my synagogue to attend daily minyan. They meditate on Friday nights and Saturday mornings and then go next door to attend Shabbat services. They meditate in the evenings before our weekly Torah study sessions. Over the years, in the course of these activities, we have used dozens of classical Jewish texts to support the integration of meditation into Jewish contexts. Laying these texts end to end, we began to see that taken as a whole they delineated a clear spiritual path of their own — a kind of soul within the body of Jewish ritual, a spiritual companion practice standing side by side with normative Judaism and supporting it, helping it to reach its full natural depth.

Be Still and Get Going presents these texts and the spiritual richness — the practice — that lies right on their surface. In doing so I hope to illuminate an indispensable resource both for Jews seeking to embrace their tradition in a deeper and more authentic way, and for anyone on the spiritual path seeking ancient wisdom for support.

THE PRACTICE POINTS

Since in my work as a teacher I have consistently stressed the primacy of daily spiritual practice, I have derived specific practice points from each chapter of this book and placed them at the end of the chapter. In the early chapters, the practice points offer detailed instructions on meditation itself. Later there are briefer and more specific exercises designed to help us focus on the particular practice issues raised by the chapter in question. This book is not intended as an exercise in theoretical theology. It is very much about practice — specifically as embedded in normative Jewish texts. I hope the practice points will serve as a guide for readers who wish to try this practice out for themselves.

Chapter One

Transformation

1. Taking Leave

WHAT IS MEDITATION?

I often ask this question at the beginning of a workshop just to get a sense of where everyone is coming from. The answers are usually quite various. Meditation is becoming still. Meditation is becoming more focused and concentrated. Meditation is becoming more aware of yourself. Meditation is becoming relaxed. Meditation is becoming more aware of God, becoming centered, becoming deeper, becoming awake. Clearly meditation is many things to people, but it is also always one thing. Meditation is always *becoming*. Meditation is always transformation. Meditation always moves us from one place to another; from unconsciousness to awareness, from tension to relaxation, from being scattered to being centered, from a shallow relationship with our environment and ourselves to a deeper one, from sleep to wakefulness, from a sense of God's absence to the sense that God was in this place all along and I didn't know it!

There's another question I usually ask at the beginning of a workshop, for similar reasons: Standing on one foot (as succinctly as you possibly can), tell me what the Torah — the five books of Moses — is all about. The answers to this question are equally various. Sunday school Jews will tell me that the Torah is the history of our people. Committed Christians and Jews will tell me that the Torah is a guide to living, a compendium of divine moral law. Jews and Christians who have spent a lot of time listening to their pastors and rabbis explicate the Bible at religious services will tell me that the Torah is about human rights and environmentalism. They will tell me it is about psychology and family relationships. They will tell me that the Torah is about whatever it was that was discussed on the op-ed page of the *New York Times* the week before.

I don't really disagree with any of these characterizations. The Torah is infinitely deep — a prism with a million faces — and does have something useful to tell us on all these subjects. But if I were to stand on one foot and tell you what the Torah was about, I would say something quite different. I would say that the Torah is the record of the human encounter with God — the transcendent, the absolute. To me this is the one capsule description that fits every page of the Torah. Every page of the Torah either describes this encounter or prepares us for it or discusses its implications. And like meditation, this encounter is always about transformation. Each encounter with God transforms us, always in a different way but always in the same way as well — by engaging us in the act of becoming who and what we are in the deepest possible sense, by carrying us through the present moment of our experience and into the measureless.

There are three texts in the Torah that describe this encounter most explicitly and at greatest length. They are the beginning of Parshat Vayetze (Genesis 28:10–19), when Jacob dreams of a ladder planted in the earth and reaching heavenward; the account of Jacob wrestling with a mysterious man in the middle of the night on the bank of the Yabok River (Genesis 32:25–33); and Moses's famous vision of the burning bush and his ensuing conversation with God about it (Exodus 3:1–16). Not surprisingly, these three encounter texts are also transformation texts. In fact each describes an important stage in the very kind of transformation that meditation effects in us. Not only that, but when read chronologically these three texts describe these stages of transformation in sequence — in precisely the order we are likely to experience them in meditation.

But before we get to all this, it must be pointed out that these three texts have another important element in common: the way they begin. Each of these texts begins with a significant leave-taking, and the Torah is at some pains to make sure we don't miss this point. The story of Jacob's ladder begins with the words *Vayetze Ya'akov mi-beir shavah, vayeileich haranah* — "And Jacob left Beersheba and went toward Haran." According to tradition, the Torah is the perfectly economical speech of God and never wastes a word. Yet there appear to be several superfluous words in this account of Jacob's departure from Beersheba. Last week I traveled from San Francisco to New York, and when friends asked me where I was going, I didn't say, "I am leaving San Francisco and going to New York." I simply said, "I am going to New York." I left it to them to infer from this that I was also leaving San Francisco, as it would be impossible for me to go to New York without doing so. I would have only mentioned that I was leaving San Francisco if there were something significant in the leaving itself. This passage begins "And Jacob left Beersheba" because the Torah wants to draw our attention to the leave-taking itself.

And so it is with the second text we will examine, the wrestling match between Jacob and that mysterious *ish* — that unidentified man who might be an angel, a demon, a prefiguring of Esau, Jacob's shadow self, or just a man (sometimes, after all, a man is just a man). This passage begins with Jacob dispatching his family to the other side of the Yabok River. Then we have the words *Vayivater Ya'akov levado* — "And Jacob was left alone." These words are also superfluous (if everyone else is on the other side of the river, then of course he is alone), except insofar as they point to his aloneness — to the fact that he has left everyone he knows, everyone from whom he derives a sense of safety and security.

It should also be noted that in both of these texts, Jacob is running for his life. In the first story he is running from his brother, Esau, who has threatened to kill him for stealing his birthright, and in the second, from his uncle Lavan, who has threatened to kill him twenty years later.

This motif continues in the Moses story. Here we have a kind of double leave-taking. First he leaves Egypt, running for his life from Pharaoh, who has threatened to kill him because of an Egyptian he has slain. So he flees to Midian, marries, and becomes a shepherd there, and then immediately leaves again, taking his flocks off to *achar ha-midbar* — literally, "the back of the desert," the farthest reaches of the wilderness — as far away from everyone else as he can get. Obviously the Torah is trying to emphasize his leaving once again. He doesn't just leave Egypt, he leaves Midian too, as decisively as he possibly can.

All this is because the Torah is trying to communicate to us that leave-taking itself is extremely significant. It is the prerequisite to any encounter with God. Most such encounters in the Torah, and in biblical literature, and in all the sacred literatures of the world, are preceded by a leave-taking. Very often there is no clear destination mentioned. The very first words God speaks to Abraham, the progenitor of the Jewish people, are "*Lech lecha*" — "Just leave." Leave your father's house, your birthplace, your culture, everything that has ever made you feel comfortable and secure, and go "*el eretz asher arecha*" — "to a land which I will show you later" — to a destination that I will not even trouble myself to identify for you now, because the point is simply to leave without any secure sense of destination, the point is to take a leap of faith.

Leave-taking — home-leaving — always precedes the Divine Encounter, because when we leave home, when we leave everything that is familiar to us, we leave convention, and most significantly, we leave habit, for God is never encountered in either convention or habit. God is encountered in reality, precisely the ground of *being* — the present-moment reality that convention and habit obscure. When we leave home, when we leave our habitual relationship to the world, we see things freshly, we become flush with our lives, we see reality and not the habitual idea of reality we have settled into at home. We see the thing itself and not the idea of the thing.

There was a famous experiment conducted at Princeton University during the 1960s, when Western psychologists were first beginning to "discover" meditation and the other Eastern spiritual arts. Three separate groups were hooked up to devices that measured galvanic skin response. The first was a group of ordinary Americans sitting in a room, doing nothing special. The second was a group of Siddha Yoga adepts in the midst of a meditative trance. The third was a group of Zen masters doing zazen — Zen mindfulness meditation. A bell was rung for each of these groups at regular intervals — every fifteen or thirty seconds — and their responses were measured. The first group, the ordinary citizens sitting around in a room, registered a very strong response to the first ringing of the bell, a somewhat weaker response to the second ringing, and then an increasingly diminishing response to each subsequent ringing. Finally they registered no response at all. The bell continued to ring at regular intervals, but as far as the people in this room were concerned, it might as well not have been ringing at all. They had become habituated to the sound, and it was as if it weren't there. This in fact is how we live much of our lives. We become so habituated to our experience that we stop processing it at all. It is as if it weren't there, or as if we weren't there experiencing it.

Just for the record, the Siddha Yogis, in trance meditation, never registered any response at all, not even to the first ringing of the bell. They were entirely elsewhere the whole time. The Zen masters, on the other hand, registered the maximum possible response — complete shock — with every ringing of the bell. They never became habituated to their experience. Their mindfulness seemed to put them in a permanent state of leave-taking, unwaveringly flush with their experience.

My wife is a novelist. Her first novel, *This Flower Only Blooms Every Hundred Years*, was a record of every vacation she had ever taken in her life. She decided on this narrative strategy because she realized that when you are on vacation, you are subject to neither the conventions and habits of the place you are visiting, nor the conventions and habits of the place you have left. That's why we love vacations so. Free of convention and habit, we are flush with our experience. Things seem vivid and fresh. Life stops rushing by beneath our radar screen and we actually begin to feel it.

Krishnamurti, the great Indian philosopher and spiritual teacher, used to recommend a rather strange practice, which I actually perform from time to time to the consternation of everyone I know. Whenever anyone asks us a question — even the simplest question imaginable, like "What's your favorite color?" or "What kind of music do you like?" — we should train ourselves to respond immediately with the phrase "I don't know." Otherwise we find ourselves trotting out habitual answers, not the way we feel or think at the moment, but the way we felt or thought long ago.

Perhaps someone asks us how we feel about capital punishment. Usually we do not really answer that question at all. In all likelihood we have no idea how we feel about capital punishment at the moment, because whenever someone asks us we trot out the brilliant answer we formulated fifteen years ago — our habitual answer, one that worked very well back then and continues to dazzle whenever we pull it out. But as brilliant as it may be, it is obscuring how we feel about the matter now, the answer to that question which is waiting to arise in this moment. We need to effect a leave-taking. If we want to discover how we feel and what we think about capital punishment now, we have to let go of that brilliant answer. We have to say "I don't know" and spend a moment or two in the void, having let go of our old habitual, secure response, and having no idea what will arise in its place. This is the only way we can get at the truth of the moment, the only way we can continue to grow and evolve.

Passover, the time of the great liberation (the exodus from Egypt), and Shavuot, the time of the great revelation (the giving of the Torah at Mount Sinai), are connected by a period of fifty days — a week of weeks plus one day more — which we count in ritual fashion, in order to bind the first holiday to the second. Why do we do this? According to the Sefat Emet, the great Hasidic commentator, we connect the time of our liberation to the time of our revelation because the revelation we experience on Shavuot is precisely proportional to the liberation — the leave-taking — we experience on Passover. We have to let go of yesterday's Torah — the Torah we know by habit and rote — in order to make room for the Torah peculiar to this moment, the particular truth we can only know when we have left habit and convention behind and are flush with our experience. This, according to the Sefat Emet, is why we empty our house of *chametz* — of leavened grains and by extension all grain products — in the days preceding Passover. This emptying — this letting go of the flour that has become stale — is a tangible representation of the spiritual liberation we hope to achieve. We must leave, we must let go of that which is stale, in order to make room for that which is fresh and new and arising out of this moment.

But the characters in these biblical texts do not just leave, they run. Specifically they run for their lives. Jacob runs away because Esau wants to kill him, and twenty years later he runs away because Lavan wants to kill him; and Moses runs away from Pharaoh, who wants to kill *him*. Why are these people running for their lives? I once asked this question at a workshop I was conducting with my good friend Sylvia Boorstein. She had a wonderful answer. According to Sylvia, they are running for their lives because without this kind of direct and mindful experience of our lives, it is as if we are dead. The bell continues to ring, but it is as if we are not there, as if we are not experiencing our lives, as if our lives are going on without us. So we see these biblical figures taking leave of a kind of living death. Entombed in habit and convention, they are dead to their lives. Taking leave, they are literally running *for* their lives — toward their lives — rushing toward an embrace of their actual present-tense experience.

I think there is something else going on here too. I think we see all these figures taking their leave at gunpoint, as it were, because no sane person ever voluntarily leaves the places and things that make him feel comfortable and secure. We leave the comfortable, the secure, the habitual, only when forced to do so, and the proximate cause of our leaving is very often a matter of life and death. What is it that usually disrupts our habitual patterns and brings us face-to-face with our lives? Some crisis, some trauma, often of the life-threatening sort. We lose a loved one, or we are faced with a life-threatening illness ourselves. We lose a job, or our spouse leaves us. These are the kinds of events that usually lead us to a radical break with the pat assumptions of our lives. We don't make this kind of break for fun.

Spiritual activity such as meditation replicates leave-taking for us. Simply to begin to meditate is to leave the way we ordinarily live, and every conscious expulsion of breath is a leave-taking of sorts as well. But this activity in and of itself is unlikely to bring us to the real point of departure. Only life itself and the incredibly powerful disruptive forces it inevitably carries with it seem capable of doing that. The point of spiritual practice, I think, is simply to prepare us for the great moments of leave-taking life will bring us, and to help us make constructive use of them. The traumas and crises of life don't automatically bring us to the point of a spiritual breakthrough. They are just as likely to crush and embitter us. Spiritual practice helps us to identify the moments of crisis as opportunities for leave-taking, for being flush with our lives again, for seeing the world afresh, for encountering God.

A few final words about the leave-taking theme: As I mentioned earlier, this is not a phenomenon peculiar to either the Bible or to Judaism. Leave-taking is a universal prerequisite to the encounter with God. It is part of the archetypal human religious experience. In all the religions of the world, we see a single figure taking leave, going off by himself, quite often into the wilderness, and experiencing the transcendent there. He then returns to the tribe, and his experience becomes the basis of a new religion.

So it was that the Buddha, driven by the discovery of suffering all around him in the world, left his parents' home, wandered the world alone, and finally found enlightenment alone beneath the Bo tree. And so it was that Jesus, after his baptism, went into the wilderness alone for forty days and forty nights and returned with a New Testament. And so it was that Muhammad fled Mecca and

went to Medina, at the farthest reaches of the Arabian desert —
achar ha-midbar — to express the prophecy that would eventually
become Islam. The Torah certainly knows this archetype. Abraham,
Jacob, and Moses are prime exemplars of it. Each goes off by himself, encounters God, and brings both the news and the perceived
consequences of the encounter back to his people.

But the seminal revelation of Judaism, the giving of the Torah
at Mount Sinai, departs from this archetypal model significantly
and in so doing advances the universal archetype. Here both the
leave-taking — the exodus from Egypt — and the revelation at
Sinai are irredeemably communal. The entire people of Israel
leaves Egypt, and the entire people of Israel receives the Torah at
Sinai, and the religion that flows out of these events will perforce
be irredeemably communal as well. From that moment at Sinai
forward, leaving the community becomes a taboo. *Al tifros min
ha-tzibor* — "Never separate yourself from the community under
any circumstances" — the rabbis of the Talmud warn us severely.
Now the idea of leave-taking needs to be reinterpreted. Now it
becomes an *inner* process. *Hitbodidut,* the Hebrew word for a
physical leave-taking, now becomes the word for meditation
instead. In other words, leave-taking no longer means that we
have to pack a suitcase and go to Philadelphia. Rather it means
that we remain in the community — whatever human community
we happen to be connected to — but engage in an activity that
helps us to take leave of our habitual way of relating to our experience. It means that we leave our usual state of scattered unconsciousness and enter a state of great concentration. In short it
means transformation, both the cause and the product of the encounter the Torah devotes itself so single-mindedly to describing —
the encounter with God.

2. God Is in This Place

Now for the transformation itself. As I mentioned earlier, there are three texts that devote more space to the encounter with God than any others. These texts also describe significant transformations, as all descriptions of the divine encounter do. Now the Torah is very kind and considerate with us. Knowing we are rather slow on the uptake, and wanting to make sure that we don't miss this very important point, the Torah employs a consistent technique — the changing of names — to draw our attention to the business of transformation. Name changes are common in the Torah. People, places, mountains and cities, and even God, frequently undergo changes in name, which point us to the significant transformation at hand. They tell us who or what has been transformed, and they hint at what kind of transformation has taken place.

In the first text, Jacob's ladder dream, it is the place — the location of Jacob's vision — that has its name changed. This place, at the borderline of the land of Canaan, was originally named Luz, but right after Jacob's vision he renames it Beit El — the House of God. The Torah is careful to prepare us for the idea that the transformation described in this text is connected with a sense of place. The land seems to be reaching out for Jacob, connecting with him deeply from the very beginning of the story. *Va-yifga ba-makom* — "And he lighted upon the place" — the Torah tells us. The root of the word *va-yifga* (and he lighted) is *faga,* which is also the word for touching. So right from the beginning of this story, Jacob and this place are involved in intimate contact: they are touching each other. The passage continues. *Va-yicach mei-avenei ha-makom* (and he took one of the stones of the place), *va-yasum m'rashoto* (and he put it under his head), *va-yischcav ba-makom ha-hu* (and he lay down in this place). The intimate embrace between Jacob and this place is expressed here quite literally. The place gives of itself to Jacob; its very stones rest under Jacob's head. Jacob and this place are intertwined. The threefold repetition of *ha-makom* or *ba-makom* — "the place" or "in the place" — roots us in the particularity of this precise spot, the very place upon which Jacob stands.

The central image of this passage stresses the same thing.

And he dreamed, and behold, a ladder, planted on the earth [*mutzav artzah*], with its head reaching toward the heavens [*v'rosho magia ha-shamaimah*], and angels, messengers from God, going up and down on it [*v'malachei Elohim olim v'yordim bo*].

This image has provoked a long history of interpretation, most of it highly symbolic. Many have seen the ladder as a symbol of the divine commandments, an apparatus that carries us heavenward step by step. Others have seen the image as one of many in the Torah that suggest the special qualities of the land of Canaan — of Israel — and particularly its capacity to bring us closer to God.

Personally I find that the images in the Torah yield the deepest meaning when interpreted as literally as possible. Think of this image for a moment. What is planted in the earth with its head reaching for the heavens? Of course it is us, the sentient creatures of this world. Though we are bound to the earth by gravity, there is nevertheless something in us that wants the sky. Go into the forest and observe the trees, the plants, the flowers, all of them rooted in the ground and reaching up for the sun at the same time. Above all, observe the human being. We are certainly *mutzav artzah*, bound both physically and existentially to our earthliness. Yet at the same time, our heads are *magia ha-shamaimah*, persistently reaching heavenward on every conceivable level. We are rooted to this earth by our physicality, our somatic needs, our sexuality, our addiction to food and to the pleasures of the body. Yet something in us aspires to heaven, something in us is always reaching beyond the limits of our earthliness, and we only ignore this heavenward impulse at our peril. It is an inevitable and irresistible part of our basic equipment, and if we don't give it its due — if we surrender to our earthliness completely — it will make us miserable, it will haunt us.

So this image of the ladder is a picture of the human condition in general, but more specifically it is a picture of a human being in meditation. When we meditate we are certainly *mutzav artzah* — we take great pains to plant ourselves on the earth, to sit in a still and balanced position with as much of our lower body touching the surface of the earth as possible. This is why people commonly meditate in the lotus or half-lotus position. In this position the maximum amount of lower-body mass is in contact with the ground, while the foot turned up on the opposite thigh locks us into place. Additionally, whether we are sitting in a chair or cross-legged on the floor, the very first adjustment we make to our posture when we begin to meditate is to tilt our pelvis forward, subtly arching the small of the back. This pelvic tilt pushes our weight forward and toward the ground, all the weight and tension in our upper body falling down to the legs and toward the earth. But at the same time, the pelvic tilt sends a strong lift upward through the center of our body, and we feel ourselves reaching for the heavens as well. We feel a lift at the sternum, a lift at the crown of the skull. With the weight and tension falling to the legs, the upper body feels light and relaxed, erect and supple, held at the balance point between tension and relaxation, held up not only by the musculature of the back, but by our energy as well, by the thrust of our hips and our pelvis.

And when we tilt the hips and pelvis forward, we open the belly for breathing. And here is where the last part of Jacob's image of the ladder — *malachei Elohim olim v'yordim bo* (messengers from God, going up and down on it) — comes in. What are these messengers from God — what is it that is constantly going up and down between heaven and earth, between the human and the divine realms? Thoughts, feelings, energy, of course! All the things we become more conscious of during meditation. But most of all, there is the breath, the ultimate, the most decisive divine message — and the most conspicuous object of our awareness during meditation as well.

In meditation we sit in acute awareness of our posture and our breath, watching the breath rise and fall either in the diaphragm or at a point just below the navel, watching our thoughts rising up and then continually falling away in the mind. And when we have been doing this for a while, our awareness begins to settle into the body, the breath, the objects of mind, and they begin to feel more vibrant to us; they begin to acquire a radiance that fills us. If we keep at it, this vibrant, radiant sense, this sense of being in a sacred space, begins to spread from our meditation — from our body, breath, and mind — to *ha-makom,* our environment, to this very place, to the world around us, and we suddenly find ourselves inhabiting a radiant, sacred world. "And Jacob awoke from his dream." And we find ourselves awaking from the dim, dull dream we have been occupying up till now, and we exclaim, as Jacob did,

"Achen, yesh Adonai ba-makom hazeh v'anochi lo yadati" — "God was in this very place all along and I didn't know it."

So it is in meditation. We inhabit this very place — we enter into intimate relation with it — we inhabit the most basic elements of our present-tense reality — our breath and our body — and we fill these things with consciousness until they glow, until they become vibrant, radiant. Then this vibrancy fills us body and mind, and we walk through the world with it, awakening every moment from the dimly lit fantasy we have been caught in until now, to a luminous, sacred world, a world suffused with the presence of God.

3. Finding Your Divine Name

The second text in this biblical triptych on transformation also involves Jacob. When last we saw him, he was fleeing Canaan because his brother, Esau, had sworn to kill him. Now, twenty years later, his uncle Lavan wants to kill him too (for good reason: Jacob has spent most of the past twenty years tricking Lavan out of two of his daughters and a good deal of his wealth), and he must flee again. This time, however, there is nowhere to go except back to Canaan, where Esau awaits him. In fact upon his arrival in Canaan, he learns that Esau is coming toward him with four hundred men, not a hopeful sign from Jacob's point of view.

Jacob's preparations for the approaching confrontation ought to be looked at even though they take place both just before and just after the text we will be focusing on. When Jacob first learns that Esau is on his way at the head of a small army, his reaction is characteristic. He will try to be duplicitous; which is to say he will try to outsmart the moment, to manipulate it by dividing it in two.

Jacob has a very large retinue: two wives, two handmaidens, thirteen children, a number of menservants and womenservants, and the extremely large flocks of goats and sheep which he spent much time and energy secreting away from Lavan. Now he divides the entire entourage in two. He puts half his wives and his handmaids, half his children, his goats, and his sheep, on one side of the Yabok River, and the other half on the other side. All right, he says to himself, Esau will wipe out one half of my family, but at least I'll still have the other half left. (We are beginning to understand why it is that everyone wants to kill this man!)

But in the middle of the night, Jacob thinks better of things. He has a kind of enlightenment. He comes to the understanding that this duplicity, this division of self with which he has been accustomed to meeting his life, isn't going to work this time, and he decides to meet Esau with a full frontal presentation of self, with his whole and undivided being instead. Now he arranges his entire entourage into a kind of mandala, an integrated representation of self, carefully presented from the outside in, in order of ascending importance — first the animals, then, after an interval, the children, arranged in ascending order of who he loves most, then the handmaids, and finally, his two wives, Leah and Rachel, and himself. It is as if he were saying, "Listen, Esau, here I am. Take it or leave it. Kill me if you want to, but this is who and what I am, for better or worse."

In fact we see Esau confronting this mandala the following day, in what has always struck me as one of the Torah's funniest scenes. We imagine Esau approaching Jacob's company seething with twenty years' accumulation of bitterness and rage. Then he comes upon the outer layer of the mandala, the goats and the sheep, arrayed at intervals for maximum effect. Nice goats! Nice sheep! he says to himself. Beyond Jacob, he sees the children, increasingly lovable as they go. Nice kids! Then he sees the handmaids, then Leah and Rachel, one woman more beautiful than the next. Beautiful handmaidens! Gorgeous wives! Finally he comes upon Jacob, standing upright at the center of this magnificent presentation, and instead of striking out at him, instead of killing him as he had no doubt intended to do, the ever-impulsive Esau now throws himself on his estranged brother, embracing and kissing him.

But in the text in question, we are still back in the middle of the previous night. Jacob has just reconsidered the division of his family into two camps and gathered them all together on one side of the Yabok. Then, as the text begins, Jacob is alone on the other side, and immediately we are told that a mysterious *ish*, an ominous, unidentified man, struggles with him, wrestles with him until the coming of the dawn. This man sees that he can't overcome Jacob, so he touches him in the hollow of the thigh and Jacob's thigh is injured. The man says, "Let me go, for the sun is coming up," but Jacob replies, "I will not let you go unless you bless me!"

Who is this mysterious stranger? Some modern scholars see him as the reflex of an ancient Near Eastern river demon who loses his power in the daylight, and while this may be interesting from a historical point of view, the deeper point, it seems to me, is that this man is a shadow figure, a creature of darkness. But whose shadow? Whose darkness? There are commentators who see this figure as Esau, and the whole dream as a prefiguring of the confrontation between Jacob and Esau that will take place the next day. And there are commentators who see the man as an angel of

God. After all, Jacob has spent his entire life struggling against the lot in life God has assigned to him, and this struggle has certainly left him wounded. But the likeliest reading, it seems to me, is that this man is Jacob's own shadow, that this is a story about Jacob confronting his own darkness.

"What is your name?" the man says to Jacob.

"Jacob," he replies.

"Your name shall no longer be called Jacob," the man announces, "but rather Israel [*Yisra-El*] for you have wrestled [*yisra*] with God [*El*] and with human beings, and you have survived."

Now what does this mean? In order to answer this question, I think we have to ask another question first: Do we like Jacob? The likely answer is that we do not. We may revere him; after all, he is one of our three ancestral patriarchs. We may even respect him; he is certainly clever, audacious, and remarkably determined. But there is something fundamentally unlikable about our ancestor Jacob. He is deceitful, manipulative, grasping, whining. He is never satisfied. He is always trying to climb out of his own experience and into someone else's, out of the present moment of his own life and into some other moment. He is always struggling with the way things are and trying somehow to have them be otherwise. And he has always been this way. His name, Jacob — in Hebrew, Ya'akov — is derived from the Hebrew word for heel, because he came out of the womb trying to supplant his older twin by grabbing his heel and pulling him back into the womb so that he could be born first. This failed, of course, so he stole first his brother's birthright and then later his blessing. He wanted to marry Lavan's younger daughter before the older, and then he spent six years conniving Lavan out of a sizable part of his flocks. To be sure, Jacob is not just a perpetrator here. He is also a victim of Lavan's deceit. Lavan, like Jacob, was a trickster. But the Torah takes pains to present the entire twenty-year contest between Jacob and Lavan as a kind of karmic retribution for Jacob's deception of his father. Jacob's response in every case until the present scene was to outtrick the trickster. And at the very end of his life, when the Pharaoh of Egypt called him in for a little small talk, Jacob unburdened himself of a most unseemly complaint. Pharaoh simply asked him how he was. "Few and evil have been the days of my life!" Jacob replied. "And they have not attained unto the days of the lives of my fathers." What a whiner! The rabbis of the Talmud really let Jacob have it for this gratuitous display of self-pity.

It should be pointed out that we are not the only ones who seem to dislike Jacob for his grasping, striving, complaining nature. Esau doesn't like him very much. Lavan doesn't like him very much. But the character who seems to dislike Jacob most of all, of course, is Jacob himself. This is why he is always trying to be someone or something he is not. He is literally uncomfortable in his own skin. In fact this expression comes from Jacob's story — from the moment when Jacob covers himself with animal skins so his father will think he is the hairy-skinned Esau and not himself.

This is why the present passage is so extraordinary and why it represents such a profound moment of spiritual transformation. The angel of God tells Jacob that the very thing he can't stand about himself — the very thing no one can stand about him — is in fact his divine name. *Yisrael* — he continually struggles with

God and with man, rails against his lot in life, tries to take that which is not his. Yet here we learn that he is this way because this is how God has made him. This is his uniqueness, the source of his power in the world, and this no doubt is precisely why he can't stand this quality in himself. It's what makes him different from others, and it's what makes him powerful, and therefore threatening to others as well.

This, I think, is the most significant moment of personal transformation we ever reach in our lives — the moment when we realize that the thing we can't stand about ourselves is our divine name; the moment when we realize that the thing about ourselves we have been avoiding, the thing we hate to see, is the very thing that makes us unique, that gives us our unique power as human beings.

This is the second stage of transformation that meditation brings about in us. In what I call Stage One Spiritual Transformation, which was described in the preceding section, we saturate the essential elements of our present-tense experience, the breath and the body, with awareness, transforming our immediate environment into a sacred, radiant place. But after we have been focusing on the breath and the body for some time, something else begins to happen, a deeper stage of transformation. It is inevitable that as we try to focus on the breath and the body — on the present moment of our experience — thoughts will arise and carry our awareness away. This is not a failure in meditation but rather an extremely important part of the process. The mind is continually producing thoughts, and sooner or later one of these thoughts will seize our attention and carry it away from the object of our concentration. If we have been meditating for thirty years, this may happen somewhat less frequently than when we first began, but it will happen nonetheless.

Herbert Benson, the Harvard physiologist, did extensive research on the psychophysiology of meditation and found that the critical moment in meditation — the moment when all the psychospiritual effects and all the brain-wave changes we associate with meditation begin to occur — is precisely the moment when we realize that thoughts have arisen and carried our awareness away, and when we resolve to bring our awareness back to the object of meditation, to the breath or the body, or whatever the center of our focus might be. If we meditate regularly, we witness this moment several times, perhaps dozens of times, every day. We see the thoughts and feelings that have carried our awareness away, and eventually we become intimately familiar with them, and we come to understand that many of them are neither random nor insignificant. They continue to carry our awareness away because they are significant — because they are things we need to look at but will not, things we need to give our attention to but do not. We won't give them our attention, so they simply take it of their own accord.

Repeatedly watching these thoughts rising up and then letting them fall away again in meditation, we come to understand them as a fundamental expression of our nature. We find that we don't have to run away from them anymore. We begin to feel the power of simply accepting our nature, of simply being who we are. We begin to stop wishing we were somehow otherwise. We begin to understand that this thing we can't stand about ourselves — this thing we can't even bear to look at — is in fact our divine name, our uniqueness, the source of our unique power. This is Stage Two Spiritual Transformation.

After being informed of his name change, Jacob begs to be told the stranger's name, but the stranger makes a cryptic response. He doesn't tell Jacob his name; he doesn't say yes, and he doesn't say no. He says, "Why do you even have to ask me my name?" And then he blesses him. What does this answer mean, and why does it lead to a blessing? The stranger is now affirming that Jacob has indeed confronted his own shadow. That's why he shouldn't have to ask the stranger's name — after all, it is his own name. And this is both his blessing and his transformation — the discovery of his real name, the reconciliation with his own darkness. His transformation allows him to reconcile with his brother as well. Reconciled with our own darkness, we stop projecting it onto our brother. Transforming our darkness into our divine name, we have no need for conflict anymore. We see, in the face of our brother, not the face of a mysterious stranger, not a threatening adversary, but the face of God. So it is that this text concludes, "And Jacob called the name of the place Peniel [*p'nei*=face; *El*=God]: for I have seen God face to face and my life is preserved." And the next day, when he and Esau, his sworn enemy, finally meet, he exclaims once again, "I have seen your face as one sees the face of God."

4. Finding God in the Present Moment

In the first text, the name of the place was changed from Luz to Beit El, signaling that Jacob's consciousness of his environment, of the world he inhabits, has been transformed. In the second text, Jacob's own name was changed, signaling that his consciousness of himself has been transformed. In the third text, the story of Moses and the burning bush, it is God's name that is changed, mirroring the third significant stage in meditative transformation — when our consciousness of God is transformed.

Until now we have made mention of God several times without really saying much about what we were talking about. We spoke of a sense of the presence of God in the world around us — God is in this very place and I didn't even know it — and we spoke of coming to see the face of God in our own nature and in the face of our brother or sister too. It is just as well that we didn't say much about God in speaking of these earlier texts. The truth is, in the early stages of the spiritual path, we may sense the presence of God but we really don't know much, if anything, about what we are sensing. Here in the story of the burning bush, however, we do begin to discover something about the nature of this presence we have only been able to blindly intuit up till now.

Having taken his leave of everyone he knows, the shepherd Moses now finds himself *achar ha-midbar*, alone in the farthest reaches of the desert. Finally he comes to Horeb, the mountain of God, and there he sees a strange apparition, identified again as *malach Elohim* — an angel, or a messenger of God. Here the apparition takes the form of a flame within a bush. As Moses continues to stare at the bush, he notices that the fire is burning unabated but the bush is not being consumed. Moses's interest is piqued. "I'm going to turn around now," he says, "to get a better look at this great apparition, this bush which is burning without being consumed." And when God sees that Moses is turning around, God calls out, "Moses! Moses!" from the midst of the bush, and Moses says, *"Hineni"* — "I am here, God," I am standing before you, prepared to do your will.

One of the things that has always puzzled me about this passage is this business of turning around. Why does Moses turn around, and why does his turning seem to provoke God to call out his name? One of the best interpretations of this passage I have ever read was written by Richard Maurice Bucke, a nineteenth-century Canadian psychiatrist and a spiritual disciple of the poet Walt Whitman. Whitman was a guru of sorts in his own time, and Bucke was one of his most ardent followers. Bucke wrote a book called *Cosmic Consciousness,* a kind of pseudoscientific study of enlightened spiritual awareness. In this book Bucke endeavored to record every known instance of encounter with the Cosmic Sense, borrowing from all the sacred literatures of the world, from poetry, and from the private letters of mystics and theosophists of his own time. He included the story of Moses and the burning bush to illuminate a particular facet of this experience.

According to Bucke, instances of cosmic consciousness often begin with a sudden eruption of inner light so vivid that the person experiencing it is convinced that the light is coming from outside himself, that it is an objective phenomenon that exists in the outside world. How does someone come to realize that a light he thought was external is really internal? According to Bucke, we discover this by turning around, just as Moses did. We see a light on the wall in front of us, we turn to the right and the light is still in front of us, and we realize that the light is not outside us but within; we realize that it is an inner light, the light of God. So it is that when Moses begins to turn around — when he begins to understand that this experience of light is taking place inside himself and not in the bush — he suddenly hears the voice of God calling his name. He answers, and God begins to speak.

The first thing God has to say is straight out of Stage One Spiritual Transformation: "Take off your shoes, because the place [again *ha-makom*] you are standing is sacred ground." Then God begins to tell Moses that he has a mission, an echo of the second stage. We come out of the encounter with God with a glimmer of our divine name, with a sense of mission, with the sense that our lives have meaning, and perhaps even an inkling of what that meaning might be. Here Moses learns that his mission is to go back to Egypt and bring out all the Jews.

Please imagine for a moment what you would feel like if God appeared to you in a burning bush and told you that you had to go back to New Jersey and bring out all the Jews. How would you respond? Probably very much the way Moses did. You would raise a number of very impassioned objections. Are you kidding? Who is going to believe me? I'm not capable of doing such a thing, et cetera, et cetera. As Moses raises these objections and as they are answered one by one, Moses is plunged into Stage Two Spiritual Transformation — he is forced into a painful confrontation with his own sense of inadequacy and then beyond that to a sense of his real power as a human being and his mission in life. Along the way he arrives at Stage Three.

If you were to go back to New Jersey and suggest to the good Jewish people there that God wants them to leave and go out into a frightening wilderness, among the many things they might ask you (while they were waiting for the attendants from the local mental hospital to arrive) is "What God? What are you talking about? Who is this God you say wants us to leave New Jersey?" Moses anticipates this particular question. "When I go to the Children of Israel," he says, "and I say to them, the God of your ancestors has sent me to you, and they say to me, 'What is his name?' what shall I say to them?"

God's answer to this question is, I believe, the single most important piece of information the Torah ever imparts to us. *"Ehiyeh asher ehiyeh"* — "I will be as I will be," God replies. But the verb *ehiyeh* is a very strange verb in Hebrew, a rendering of the verb "to be" in a flowing tense partaking of past, present, and future, so that God's reply might just as easily be rendered "I was as I was" or "I am as I am." What God seems to be saying to Moses here is, "My name — my essential nature — is absolute and unconditioned being in the present moment; absolute and unconditioned becoming, past, present, and future; absolute existence in the great, eternal moment."

Every language is also a theology. It is one of the peculiarities of the Hebrew language that there is no way of expressing the verb "to be" in the present tense, except for the name of God. If we want to say "I am tall" in Hebrew, we can really only say "I tall." God is the only am what am. The implication of this linguistic oddity is that God is the only thing that can be absolutely present, and if we think about it for a moment we see that this implication is entirely correct. We ourselves can never be absolutely present. Even in those exceedingly rare moments when we are not daydreaming — when we are attending to our actual experience — we are not really quite there. It takes several hundredths of a second for our nervous system to process our experience. So even when we appear to be completely flush with our experience, we are not. Even when we are inhabiting our life as fully as we can, we are not really seeing our life, but rather a movie of what happened to us several hundredths of a second ago. We can only *approach* the experience of being absolutely present, we cannot attain it. But as we do approach it, we approach God as well.

The most powerful exercise I know for approaching the present moment is, of course, meditation. In meditation we try to let go of all thoughts and feelings extraneous to the moment. We come to understand that the present moment is the only place we can experience our life, the only place we can enjoy it, the only place we can feel it. Breathing in, we enter the present moment as deeply as we can. Breathing out, we let go of everything outside this moment. Breathing in, we enter the present moment; breathing out, we feel ourselves to be a part of the timeless flow of life. The present moment is immeasurable and eternal. Past and future disappear. Past and future are contained in every breath. Every joy, every trauma we have ever experienced is here in our body and our breath; every breath carries us closer to God and the impenetrable moment of Absolute Being. Every breath carries us further along on the great journey that has no attainable destination, the great flow that has no end.

PRACTICE POINTS

Taking Leave

Every day we should set aside a fixed time for leaving our usual way of being in the world, our usual consciousness; for entering a more focused and awake relationship to our experience. Every day we should leave our usual scattered mental state and center our awareness on our body and our breath, breaking our habitual way of sitting and breathing by inhabiting these activities with awareness. The emphasis here is on *every day*. The habit of unconsciousness is very strong. Breaking free of it requires a strong, persistent effort. Real transformation requires daily practice and reinforcement. If we are truly to make ourself open and vulnerable, if we are to experience our life in a fresh and vibrant way, we must practice doing so *every day*. The crush of habit and convention is relentless. Effort and discipline are required to overcome it.

A particular kind of place is also required. Our time in meditation should be characterized by clarity, silence, and stillness. The room or area we sit in should be uncluttered and clear. The mind takes on the qualities and shapes it is surrounded by. A cluttered, disorderly space leads to a cluttered, disorderly mind. We should take off our shoes and loosen our belt as we begin. The feet are sensory organs. Bare feet help us inhabit our physical environment more deeply. The first thing God said to Moses at the burning bush was, "Take off your shoes, because the place you are standing is sacred ground." We also want our bellies to be open, because the belly is an important center of both breathing and consciousness. When our breathing is confined mostly to the chest, we take in the world in a shallow way. When our breathing engages the belly as well, we take in the world very deeply.

Silence and stillness are also important to the leave-taking we are trying to accomplish in meditation. We are trying to leave the world of unfocused chatter and constant, compulsive, reactive movement. Silent, we find ourselves entering a deeper, more tranquil world. Still, we step outside the stimuli of our lives; we stop reacting to them for a moment and so become able to see them. We can't see the picture as long as we are in it. Silent and still, we step out of the picture. What movement is necessary should be careful, quiet, conscious movement. Going to and from our seat, we should walk softly and mindfully on the balls and heels of our feet.

Since there are few things we do in life with a stronger sense of habit than sitting, it is crucial that when we sit in meditation, we sit in a conscious, focused way. It makes no difference if we sit on the floor or in a chair, but the choice is an important one in that we should sit in a position we are reasonably sure we can maintain without moving for half an hour or so. If we are sitting in a chair, we should be particularly careful not to just slouch in our habitual position. Rather we should sit with full intention, letting the spine stand freely, unsupported by the back of the chair. It is also helpful to sit toward the edge of the seat with our feet flat on the floor and balanced in front of us. The soles of our feet have wonderful mechanisms — balancing balls — and can help us find a secure and stable posture in our chair.

On the floor, we can sit in the lotus (each foot turned at the ankle and resting on the opposite thigh) or the half lotus (one foot so turned and rested, the other foot resting under the opposite thigh instead of on top of it), in the Burmese position (legs crossed, knees on floor, feet centered on the floor just in front of the genital area, one foot directly behind the other), or in the cezah (knees bent in front of us, shins flat on the floor, and ankles tucked beneath our seat). The important thing is that our knees should be lower than our hips or at least on the same level. Otherwise we will not be able to make the pelvic tilt we mentioned earlier (and will mention again below). Unless we are extremely limber, if we are sitting on the floor we will require a cushion (at least one) to achieve this.

Although this might sound paradoxical for an exercise in leave-taking, I think it's important to sit with other people, if not

every day, then at least whenever possible. Meditation is very difficult. It forces us to look at things we have invested a lot of energy
in not seeing. We will inevitably reach the point where our resistance to this process will become so great we will want to quit. The
support of others is crucial at such times. There have been many
times when my own meditation has led me to such difficult moments that I would have gotten up and left the room if I hadn't
been too embarrassed to do so in front of others. Moreover, one of
the states we are most interested in leaving behind is the exaggerated sense of self — the delusion that we are discrete, isolated
entities — that afflicts so many of us. Sitting in meditation with
others — breathing the same air, hearing the same sounds, thoughts
rising and falling in the same patterns — we experience ourselves
to be deeply connected to one another, the constituents of a single,
interpenetrating whole, and this sense of things is perhaps the most
significant leave-taking we can make.

Planted on the Earth, Reaching Toward the Heavens

Whether we are sitting in a chair or on the floor, the first thing we
want to do in preparing for meditation is to tilt our pelvis and our
hips slightly forward. When we do this we feel a gentle pressure
pushing our knees down toward the ground, weight and tension
falling into the legs and the lower body, all of which enhances our
sense of being rooted in the earth. (This downward pressure will
be most apparent to those who sit on the floor, but it can also be
achieved in a chair by raising the back legs of the chair an inch or so.)
At the same time, this pelvic tilt sends a distinct lift up the center of
the upper body. We feel this lift at the sternum and at the crown of
the skull as well. Meditation is an *active* state. This sense of reaching

upward toward the sky makes us feel as if we are holding the upper body aloft with energy as well as with the musculature of the back.

As we tilt the pelvis and hips forward, the upper body is balanced, held at an equipoise, erect but supple, relaxed and alert. As weight and tension fall into the lower body and legs, the upper body becomes light and relaxed. The head should be held up, ears aligned with the shoulders and chin tucked very slightly toward the collarbone. This aligns the upper spine with the rest of it. Proper alignment is very important because of the spine's vital role as a conduit of nerves, nerve endings, and energy. The mouth should be closed, the teeth open and unclenched. The eyes should be half opened, without focusing on the visual field. If we close the eyes we will be tempted to fall into a dream or a trance. If we look at the objects of sight, we will distract ourselves from the inner objects of our concentration.

Body and mind should be held at the same balance point we mentioned above — between relaxation and tension, relaxed but alert, supple but erect. To this end, the hands should be held in a conscious position — either in an oval on the lap (thumbs touching on the top, fingers overlapped on the bottom), or resting palm up on the knees, with the thumb and forefinger of each hand forming a circle. We can then monitor the hands to make sure that they are neither clenched nor slack. The connection between the hands and the mind is very strong. The mind tends to follow the hands, and the body follows the mind. If the hands are held at this balance point, both mind and body will tend to follow.

And Messengers from God
Going Up and Down

The most important consequence of tilting the pelvis and hips forward is that it opens the belly for breathing, thus allowing the breath to penetrate deeply and naturally. With the posture properly assumed, and the mind gently monitoring it during meditation, periodically checking to see that spine, hips, pelvis, hands, sternum, skull, head, and so on are still correctly positioned, we begin to allow our awareness to settle gently into our breath. We bring our focus in from all the places where it is usually scattered, to the diaphragm, the center of our breathing, the muscle located several inches above the navel.

The breath does not need to be controlled, but it may need to be assisted to penetrate deeply into the body. It is the movement of the diaphragm, in concert with the muscles of the chest, that regulates the expansion and contraction of the lungs. This expansion and contraction is augmented when the belly is also involved in the action of breathing. The belly is a center of spiritual consciousness. Consciously using the belly to help draw air deeply into the body activates this center and allows us to experience the world in a fuller way.

It may be helpful to begin this period of mindful breathing by expanding the belly, making it big like a beach ball to allow the lungs to expand more fully, then letting the air out very slowly. We can do this for half a dozen breaths or so and then let the breath simply flow naturally, gently watching the diaphragm as the breath moves in and out. Or we may begin by following the full course of the breath in some detail. We can watch the breath as it comes into the nostrils; follow the inhale as it descends down the breathing tube into the lungs; imagine the belly filling with breath; attend to the subtle moment when the inhale becomes an exhale; follow the full course of the exhale from the belly to the nostrils; and then attend to that small moment of faith when the breath leaves the body altogether and then returns again of its own accord, without any conscious activity on our part. Again, we need only do this for half a dozen breaths or so. After that we can just watch the breath rise and fall at the diaphragm in a much gentler and more general way.

When we are settled into a natural, rhythmic pattern of breathing, we can let the momentum of the in-breath bring our attention in from all the mental corners where it is usually scattered and focus it at the center of our breathing. We can let the momentum of the out-breath help us to relax very deeply; to let go of tension, both muscular and emotional; to let go of regret about things that have already happened; to let go of anxiety about things that haven't happened yet; focusing as we breathe in, letting go as we breathe out. As our awareness begins to permeate the breath and the body, they begin to glow as if lit from within. The breath begins to bring a wonderful calm to the body, a radiant calm that fills us body and mind.

Finding Our Divine Name

As we try to focus on the breath and the posture, our mind will inevitably wander. Thoughts, bodily sensations, noises, and visual stimuli arise, and sooner or later these things carry our awareness away. This is in no way a failure in meditation. Rather it is part of the process. The critical moment in meditation, in fact, is when we realize that this has happened — that our awareness has been carried away by a thought or a sensation. Then we simply take note of the thought that has carried us away, let it rise up as it needs to do, let it fall away again — as it will if we don't hold on to it — and then gently bring our awareness back to the breath and the body.

Over time we will become quite conscious of the thoughts that tend to carry our awareness away. After all, we witness them doing so dozens of times during each meditation. Particular thoughts may seem random, mundane, and insignificant, but when we observe them over time, we see that they form patterns, patterns that point us to unconscious psychological truths we very much need to become conscious of. This is one of the great values of meditation. Over a long period of time, we witness our unconscious thoughts carrying our awareness away time after time, and our true nature — the way we really are as opposed to the way we would like to think of ourself — begins to emerge. We begin to learn the name God has given us, our essential self. We begin to see that the way we really are is more powerful than the way we thought we should be. We begin to understand that those things we didn't want to see about ourself are really the source of our unique power.

The Place You Are Standing Is Sacred Ground

After time, the concrete objects of focus — the breath and the particular points of our posture — begin to fall away, and our effort becomes simply to enter the present moment of our experience. Those things we were focusing on were simply the lineaments of the present moment, its most fundamental and accessible elements. Now we allow every breath to carry us deeper and deeper into the moment itself. Breathing in, we enter the present moment. Breathing out, we settle into it, we enjoy it, we feel it.

This moment is the only life we have — the only place we can live our life, feel it, experience it. Sitting still in silence, we feel a sense of timelessness. Present, past, and future dissolve in the eternal present, a boundless field of mind in which we feel our connection to everything and everyone in the range of our experience. This boundless, eternal realm is the realm of God. Approaching it, we approach God.

Chapter Two

Suffering

1. The Uses of Suffering

MOST OF US, I THINK, TEND TO THINK OF THE SPIRITUAL
path in terms of the high points: a birth, a death, that moment of
transcendence we felt during a great storm or standing by a waterfall or viewing a sunset on a trip to the mountains. But the truth is,
neither thunderbolts nor visions of pink clouds are the primary
engine of the spiritual quest; suffering is.

Certainly Buddhism recognizes this. The problem of suffering is central to both Buddhist theology and practice. The most
fundamental doctrine in Buddhism is the Four Noble Truths. The
First Noble Truth is that suffering is endemic to human existence.

To be human is to experience suffering. Nor do you have to be a Buddhist to recognize this truth. Whenever I present this idea to Jewish groups, there is first a wave of recognition — heads nodding as people all over the room acknowledge that suffering has certainly been central to their own lives — followed closely by sighs of relief and the almost audible thought, Thank God it's not just me!

"Birth is problematic; aging is hard; dying is also hard to bear," begins one classical formulation of the Four Noble Truths, but that is only the beginning of the bad news. Sorrow, pain, anger, grief, and despair are all both inevitable and oppressive. Having to put up with the things we dislike is painful, but no less than being apart from the things that we do like. Not getting what we want is extremely unpleasant, but not nearly as unpleasant as getting what we want and discovering that it's a great disappointment. It's not what we thought it would be, or it is what we thought it would be but the fear of losing it is stronger than any pleasure we might derive from having finally achieved it. In short, our experience is irredeemably unsatisfactory.

The Second Noble Truth tells us why. We inevitably experience life as suffering — as unsatisfactory — because we are afflicted with an inherent desire to have things be otherwise. No particular state is inherently afflictive. A physical or mental state only becomes so when we wish it to be some other state. If we have a pain in our leg, it only becomes suffering by virtue of our wish not to have a pain in our leg. This may be a perfectly reasonable wish, but it is not a necessary one. We might just as easily choose to see the sensation in our leg as just that — a sensation — in which case we would not experience it as suffering. Our life consists of an endless procession of sensations, thoughts, impulses, feelings. It is only our desire to hold on to some of them and to get rid of others that causes us to suffer, yet we do desire these things and we suffer as a consequence.

So far the news from the front has been pretty grim. Both suffering and the desire that causes it seem to be inescapable components of existence. But the Third Noble Truth brings us some good news. The desire that creates the sense in our psyche that all our experience is somehow unsatisfactory can be eliminated, leading to the cessation of suffering. The way to the annihilation of desire is the Fourth Noble Truth, which consists of the Eightfold Path. If we practice Right View, Right Intention, Right Speech, Right Action, Right Livelihood, Right Effort, Right Mindfulness, and Right Concentration, our desire, and consequently our suffering, will be extinguished. This sounds like a wonderfully simple plan of action, does it not? But before we break out the champagne and begin to celebrate our liberation from suffering, it should be noted that there have been dozens of schools and styles of Buddhism over the past twenty-five hundred years, and no two of them have agreed as to precisely what constitutes Right View, Right Intention, Right Action, and so forth. So apparently it isn't as simple as it seems.

Nevertheless, for all the differences as to the particulars of the Eightfold Path, there has been some consensus among most Buddhists that meditation is an important and possibly an essential element of this path. After all, if the problem is dissatisfaction with our experience, then meditation, which tends to make our experience considerably more satisfactory, would logically point toward a solution. In meditation our experience tends to become more vibrant, richer, more alive, and our desire to have things be otherwise is therefore diminished.

The amelioration of suffering is *not* the central imperative of Judaism. The central imperative of Judaism, I believe, is to recognize and manifest the sacred in everything we do and encounter in the world. While this in no way conflicts with the idea of ameliorating suffering — in fact I think we can safely assume that if we realized the sacred in the moment, we would be rather less inclined to wish that we were in some other moment — it is clearly not the same idea. Yet even if the problem of suffering is not the central concern of Jewish sacred literature, it certainly occupies a prominent place in it. In fact the very first story we tell as a people is about a man and a woman who had everything they could possibly want, but whose desire for the one thing they could not have thrust them into a world of suffering and death. I am speaking, of course, of the story of Adam and Eve in the Garden of Eden.

Kabalistic cosmology also expresses the idea that creation is fundamentally broken and that suffering is therefore inevitable. According to Lurianic Kabala, God originally existed as the Ain Sof, literally, the Endlessness — God's essential, undiluted nature, a vast and limitless emptiness so powerful, so charged with supernal energy, that nothing could coexist with it. So when God wished to bring creation into existence, it was first necessary for God to remove him/herself from a tiny dot at the center of the Ain Sof. This tiny dot became creation, the entire universe as we know it. The process of self-removal was called *tzim-tzum*, or contraction. It was accomplished by means of *kelim*, vessels that carried the Divine Light out of this tiny speck at the center of the Ain Sof. But as *tzim-tzum* unfolded, a cosmic catastrophe occurred. The Divine Light proved to be too strong for the vessels, and the vessels broke open, filling the universe with dangerous shards of devouring light, with failure, suffering, and death. The task of humanity — of all being — from the moment of that catastrophe forward became *tikun olam,* the repair of the universe, the mending of the broken vessels, and the restoration of the Divine Light to its rightful place.

But these three stories — the Four Noble Truths, the Garden of Eden, the Breaking of the Vessels — and the basic skeletal structure upon which all three of them rest, have always raised a number of troubling questions for me. Is the universe essentially deficient and in need of improvement? Is God flawed? Why was this desire which would prove to be our undoing implanted in our souls in the first place? Why did God make vessels that would break? Was God a screwup?

Or is there something about the process of healing — of working through suffering and death, of mending a broken world — that is both necessary and good? Is there something about the process of extinguishing desire that might in fact leave us better off than if we'd never had desire at all? The fall from Eden cast us out of paradise, but it also thrust us into history. Perhaps there is something necessary, even redemptive, about the experience of history. As for the Breaking of the Vessels, the rabbis of the Talmud said that it is far better to have sinned and repented than never to have sinned at all, and in the Talmudic discussion that followed this assertion, the rabbis observed (with impeccable biological correctness, it should be added) that a bone that has been broken and healed is far stronger than a bone that has never been broken.

All of this raises more questions. Suffering may very well be inevitable, but can it also be useful? Is the history we were thrust into after our fall from Eden not only inevitable but also something we needed to go through, something that benefited us more than our remaining in a static paradise would have done?

In a teaching that turns the Four Noble Truths on their collective head, Rebbe Nachman, the great Hasidic master of the eighteenth century, seems to answer these questions in the affirmative. The rebbe writes:

> The strength of a person's desire is brought about by the impediments that happen to him, so when a person needs to do something, then a hindrance arises in his path. And this hindrance is for the sake of the desire; by means of the hindrance he will have greater desire to do this thing that he needs to do than he would have had, had there been no such obstacle. For whenever a person is prevented from doing something, his or her desire to do it becomes much stronger. So it is that obstacles are placed in the way of a person who needs to do something, so that his desire to do it will be increased.
>
> This is especially true in matters of holiness, because the more important the thing desired, the greater the obstacles that are presented. Consequently, when a person experiences many obstacles to the realization of some holy task, he should realize that this shows the importance of the thing desired. This is the general rule. Every obstacle is presented only for the sake of increasing desire, so that once a person has a great desire to do something, he will carry it out; the potential will become actual.
>
> — *Likutey Ma-haran*, number 66

According to Rebbe Nachman, there is an inevitable relationship between our desire for a thing and the obstacle that stands in our way. If we didn't want a thing, we wouldn't see what was preventing us from obtaining it as an obstacle. Although the Buddhists don't acknowledge the existence of God (nor do they deny it), God — at least the God of Rebbe Nachman — seems to have a pretty good idea of how the Four Noble Truths operate. Desire causes suffering, but suffering also causes desire. If we desire that which we don't have, then suffering, in the form of an impediment to what we want, will only make us desire it more. So suffering and desire are not inherent defects in the universe, nor God's mistakes; rather they are divine instruments. And Rebbe Nachman sees this use in suffering; it can awaken us to the spiritual path and quicken our resolve to remain on it as well.

Indeed suffering can often be an awakening to the way things really are, a pathway to a clearer vision of our lives. What we call suffering is often just the differential between how life really is and how we wish it to be. A woman came to me recently. She was married to a man who had two teenaged daughters by a previous marriage. His first wife had been quite unstable and had left the children in his custody, and this woman, whom I will call Eve, had done the lion's share of mothering for the two girls and had come to love them profoundly. Occasionally the girls' birth mother would swoop down and reclaim them for a time. Eventually she would abandon them again, but they were never able to get over the hope that someday she would stay with them for good. All of this made Eve terribly anxious. She experienced the mother's behavior as a source of endless suffering. It left her feeling terribly insecure about the girls' affections, and she was sometimes terrified of losing them altogether. But when we looked at things more closely, it seemed clear that she had always been insecure about her relationship with the girls, always threatened by the possibility of losing them. After all, she wasn't really their mother, and this was quite apparent — often painfully so — to everyone involved. The mother's behavior hadn't created these feelings; it had merely brought them to light, to the surface of Eve's life. When Eve was able to see this, the mother's behavior became much less threatening to her. It was no longer a source of suffering so much as it was something that illuminated a difficult but important reality of her life.

Torah commentators have often expressed their bewilderment at the nature of the biblical affliction called *metzorah*. This word is usually translated as "leprosy," but the disease described in such detail in the book of Leviticus bears no resemblance to the modern condition of the same name, nor to any other diseases we are presently aware of. Nor do we know of any disease that takes the course that biblical leprosy took; it began in the skin of the body, and if it wasn't acknowledged and cleansed, it spread first to one's clothing and then to one's house. If our biblical ancestors failed to take care of it even then — if they failed to call in a priest to inspect their house, or to immerse themselves in the purifying waters of the ritual bath — the house had to be dismantled brick by brick.

The rabbis of the Talmud also found all of this unrecognizable from a medical point of view, so they decided that it must not have been a physical condition at all but rather a spiritual condition with physical manifestations. Why did our biblical ancestors suffer from this strange affliction while we do not? It must have been, the rabbis of the Talmud decided, that the people of the biblical era lived in such a pure spiritual state that their spiritual dysfunctions immediately manifested themselves in the material realm, first in their bodies, then in their clothing, and finally in their houses. If they acknowledged their spiritual difficulties in the first instance, the physical manifestation stopped there and didn't spread any further.

This system really was a blessing, a great gift from God, the rabbis decided, and I think they had a point. Imagine how much easier our lives would be if our spiritual and emotional problems immediately manifested themselves as a rash on our skin, instead of remaining hidden in the inner recesses of our souls and our psyches as they do now. Although acute or chronic pain can sometimes be unbearable, generally speaking, physical suffering is easier to deal with than a similar level of spiritual or emotional distress, and it is certainly easier to locate and to focus on.

I was a serious practitioner of Zen meditation for ten years, meditating for several hours a day. For the first three or four years, physical pain and suffering were the primary objects of my attention during meditation. My body wasn't very flexible, and I had a fairly unsophisticated understanding of what pain was and how to relate to it. Sitting for hours on end every day caused considerable pain in my legs and my back and especially my knees. After some years my body became more limber and my understanding of pain more subtle, and pain ceased to be the major concern of my meditation, until finally I was hardly aware of it at all. But boy did I miss it then. Meditation was so much easier when I could focus on the clear and unambiguous reality of the pain in my legs. It riveted me to the present moment. It neatly encapsulated the suffering of my life, and it was easy to concentrate on (in fact, it was almost impossible to ignore). When it was gone, I had to try to come to terms with diffuse, quicksilver mental states — with emotional confusion and spiritual entropy — that were far more elusive, less defined, and more difficult to work with.

Another thing I learned from the pain I experienced in meditation was that suffering can be a pathway to a deeper relationship with our experience. When I was talking about the Second Noble Truth, I mentioned that if we have a pain in our leg, it only becomes suffering if we wish things to be otherwise, if we wish not to have a pain in our leg. I did not come up with that example at random. This was my experience during those years of meditation when I was preoccupied with physical pain. When I was really able to be with the pain, to stop wishing it away, to stop praying for the bell to ring and put me out of my misery; when I was fully able to inhabit the sensation coming up from my knees, it ceased to be painful. Instead I found that the sensation that I had originally identified as pain had carried me into a deeper dimension of experience, a more beautiful and primary dimension where bodily sensations were like colors or waves.

I think this is generally true of our pain and suffering, physical, emotional, and spiritual. When we are trying to get away from them, our experience is relatively thin and painful, but when we confront them directly, when we acknowledge them and inhabit them as deeply as we can, our lives seem to deepen accordingly, and it becomes clear that the suffering itself has been the instrument of this deepening.

Another way of speaking about the way the suffering in our life can carry us into a deeper and richer realm of experience is in terms of leave-taking. In our discussion in the first chapter of this book, we observed that leave-taking is usually the beginning of the spiritual path. Habit and comfort place us at a distance from our experience. So the spiritual path begins when we leave behind everything that makes us feel comfortable and secure and enter a state of vulnerability and openness. It is in this state that the encounter with the transcendent is possible.

But as we also observed, no sane person leaves the things that make her feel comfortable and secure. Inevitably she is driven to leave these things by suffering. Jacob and Moses left home because someone had threatened to kill them. Muhammad was hounded out of Mecca. The Buddha left his parents' home precisely because of suffering, not only his own but everyone's. His parents had tried to protect him from suffering by walling him off in the family palace. But one day the Buddha slipped out. On the streets he found that the world was teeming with suffering and death, and this was such a shock to his meticulously sheltered system that he left his parents' house vowing not to return until he had found a solution to the problem of suffering.

A man came to me recently, a brilliant and sensitive man, a successful psychiatrist in his early seventies, who had suddenly been diagnosed with a virulent and terminal brain cancer. He had an operation and a large tumor was removed, but the prognosis remained: he would certainly die within a year's time. He came to me because he had an intuition that meditation might help him cope with the ordeal he was about to go through, with the end of life, the physical pain, and the wrenching emotional experience of losing everything and everyone. So I sat with him and taught him to meditate, but it was quite clear that he already fully understood what I was telling him. He understood far better than I did, for example, that the present moment was the only time he had, that the past was just a memory and the future just an idea, and in his case a rather murky one. He knew this and was grateful for an activity that might help him expand the present moment, to make it both larger and more vivid. He saw immediately that by focusing on the breath going in and out of his body — on the rise and fall, the systole and diastole — he was participating in the rhythm of the universe. He understood that everything in the world, including himself, was constantly rising up and falling away, and he saw that mindfully taking part in this rhythm as it manifested itself in his breath and body could make him more comfortable with the larger falling away he was now in the midst of. He saw how his anxiety and regret were impulses that, having risen up, could also fall away if he didn't hold on to them. And he fully sensed the potential of mindful meditation to transform his physical pain into something deeper.

In short he was a man who seemed to have been fully awakened by his suffering. His cancer had clearly been a leave-taking; it had brought him flush with his experience, with the truth of his life, and with its transcendent meaning as well. The fact is, while I was fairly sure meditation would be helpful to him, I wasn't sure he really needed it. In meditation we take leave of our ordinary way of being in the world, our scattered, unfocused, habitual state, and we enter into a more concentrated relationship with our life. My friend seemed already to have done this, and his cancer had clearly been the engine of his taking leave.

2. All This Perfection Which Is Fading into the Earth

Suffering has its uses. It can be a pathway both to a clearer vision of our lives and to a deeper relationship with our experience. It can be the impetus for the leave-taking that might be the beginning of our real spiritual path, our authentic encounter with the transcendent. But just as clearly, we must acknowledge that there is such a thing as useless, irredeemable suffering, suffering that has no purpose we can identify nor any meaning we can possibly understand. This is the conclusion, in any case, of the passage from the Talmud that examines the question of suffering most directly, explores various possibilities as to what it might mean, and then arrives at the terrifying conclusion that there is suffering we can neither explain nor control.

This discussion begins early on in the very first tractate of the Talmud, on the fifth page of *Masecet Berachot* (Blessings). The Talmudic sage Raba gets the ball rolling with a three-part statement on the meaning of suffering and our response to it. If a person sees that afflictions have come upon him, Raba says, he should examine his behavior. Now before we get very far into this discussion, it should be observed that in considering the question of why we suffer, the rabbis are stepping into a minefield of inappropriate guilt and blame, and in order to keep from getting hopelessly lost in outrage, it might be useful for us to submit every assertion the rabbis make to two basic questions: (1) Is it ever true? Does the assertion have any validity at all? (2) Is it always true? Are we in the presence of a comprehensive answer to the question of suffering? Generally, I think, we'll find that the answer to question number one is usually yes and the answer to question two is always no.

So it is with Raba's first proposition. Is it ever true that we bring about our own suffering by our behavior, by our conduct? Of course it is! If we smoke two packs of cigarettes a day and then come down with lung cancer, we might not be groveling in inappropriate guilt if we assume there is a cause-and-effect relationship between our behavior and the suffering that has come in its wake. Do people often respond to us with defensive anger? Perhaps we have a tendency to be critical without realizing it. Perhaps there is something in our body language or our tone of voice that provokes this kind of response. So it is certainly sometimes true that our behavior brings about our suffering. Consequently, the very first thing we ought to do when suffering comes upon us is to examine our conduct to see if we have brought this suffering on ourselves.

But is it always true that our suffering is brought on by our own behavior? Of course not! When we are afflicted with illness or loss, we feel struck as if by an angry parent, and it is natural for us to assume that we must have done something wrong. But quite often we have not. Quite often illness strikes at random or for environmental causes and not because of anything we have done. Quite often people's negative responses to us are rooted in their own twisted psychologies and not in anything we have done or said to provoke them.

Raba knows this as well as we do. That's why his statement has a second and a third part. If we examine our behavior and find that we have done nothing to bring about our present suffering, Raba continues, then perhaps we can hang the whole thing on *bitul* Torah — time wasted that we might have spent studying Torah. We can either understand this to mean literally studying

Torah, or we can take it to mean spiritual practice in general. For the rabbis of the Talmud, Torah study was, after all, spiritual practice par excellence. So we are bidden to ask: Can an insufficiency in spiritual practice ever cause us to suffer? Here, I think, the answer is more complicated. Our reaction to religious fundamentalists, who often draw too clear a connection between the insufficiency of our piety and our suffering, might incline us to answer this question too quickly in the negative. Does God punish us for our religious impiety by causing us to suffer? This is both a dangerous and an unanswerable question.

But on reflection, I think, we have to admit that yes, it is sometimes true that religious practice can reduce the amount of suffering we experience. Considering this proposition on its simplest level, most religions advocate a code of moral conduct — the Judeo-Christian Ten Commandments, Judaism's 613 commandments, Theravada Buddhism's Vinaya, Mahayana Buddhism's Ten Precepts, et cetera. These codes prohibit such things as adultery, violence, dishonesty, and disrespect, all of which create a web of suffering in the world and eventually come back to us no matter how indirectly. Even factoring in for hypocrisy, it is probably true that if we follow one of these religious paths we are somewhat less likely to engage in these behaviors than we might otherwise be. And besides, if one is sincerely religious, overt hypocrisy is more difficult to pull off. For most of us, I think, the times we have said to ourselves, "This is wrong, and I know this is wrong, but I'm going to do it anyway," are relatively few, especially compared to the times we have done wrong unwittingly. Yet we can all recall at least a few such moments in our lives, and they tend to be especially damaging. When we are on a sincere religious path, such moments can become excruciating. It is rather more difficult to stand before the transcendent in the midst of our religious practice — in prayer or in meditation — when we know we have willfully acted contrary to the transcendent will. The pain this is likely to cause in our soul can be immense, and having gone through this experience once, we are unlikely to want it to happen a second time.

So let's assume that most of the things we do to bring suffering on ourselves and others, we do unconsciously. Most of the time, we stumble through our lives like a drunk stumbling through a dark attic, causing damage helter-skelter to ourselves and to others. Usually we realize we've been acting destructively after the fact, and sometimes we throw up such a daunting thicket of self-deception and justification that we never realize it at all. Many religious practices either teach or nurture a sense of mindfulness. Mindful of our actions, we tend to behave in less hurtful ways. We tend to strike out in anger somewhat less frequently, to refrain from acting on our darkest impulses somewhat more, and we suffer less as a consequence.

Perhaps the most significant way religious practice might diminish the suffering we experience is that it can change the quality of our consciousness. Even if nothing else changes in our lives, even if events we have previously experienced as suffering continue to occur, religious practice might transform our consciousness so that we no longer experience them as such, so that we understand them differently.

The high point of the High Holiday liturgy is the Une Tane Tokef prayer, a prayer that is at the same time rather exalted and rather grim. Will we live or will we die in the coming year? Our fate is written in the great books on Rosh Hashanah and sealed on Yom Kippur. On these days, in these books, it is determined who will live and who will die — who will die by violence, by flood, by fire, or by pestilence. But then comes the good news. *Teshuvah, u'tzedakah, u'tefilah ma'avirin et roat-ha-gezerah* — "Repentance [turning, returning], charitable acts, and prayer transform the evil of the decree."

This line of the liturgy derives from a passage in the Talmud that makes a similar but not identical claim. In the Talmud these spiritual activities, prayer, charitable acts, and repentance, are said to *ma'akirin et ha-gezerah* — to "tear up the decree." So it was the claim of the Talmud that if we prayed and performed charity and repented during the ten days between Rosh Hashanah and Yom Kippur, the decree of death that had been written for us could be undone; it would be torn up and we wouldn't die. But after a thousand years or so, it became quite obvious that this was simply not an accurate depiction of reality. It was plain to see that people could pray their heads off, do charity until they dropped, and make the most sincere and profound repentance imaginable and still die. In fact it was plain to see that this happened all the time. So the liturgy was rewritten to reflect reality more closely. Now the claim was that religious activities such as prayer, charity, and repentance did not necessarily avert the decree that had been written against us — these things did not change what happened. Rather they changed the way we understood what happened. These spiritual activities transformed our consciousness, so that we understood what had happened to us not as evil but simply as what had happened to us. If everything that happened to us came from God, none of it could be evil. Spiritual activities like prayer and charitable acts transformed us so that we could see this. The decree remained in force; it would not be torn up. What was meant to happen to us would still happen, but we would not experience it as evil. We would not experience it as suffering.

So is Raba's second proposition ever true? Is our suffering ever diminished by religious activity? Yes. Every religion urges conscious behavior on us which will minimize suffering; many religions teach mindfulness, which diminishes the hurtful things we do unconsciously; and spiritual activity has the potential to transform our consciousness, so that even when suffering occurs we do not experience it as such. But is Raba's second proposition always true? Of course not. Piety does not prevent people from either causing or experiencing suffering, no matter how sincere their religiosity or how transformed their awareness.

So it is incumbent upon Raba to come up with a third idea, and this one is really a beaut. If we search our souls and we find that we have done nothing to cause our suffering, and if our religious commitment is beyond reproach, then we can be confident that the suffering must be *yisurin shel ahavah* — "an affliction born of love," a suffering God has visited upon us out of his boundless love for us.

What did the rabbis mean by this? It isn't entirely clear from the long discussion that follows. At times they seem to be talking about suffering that God brings upon us for our own good or as a course correction, events that seem to be afflictions at the time but that we ultimately come to regard as blessings. Thank God that SOB fired me, we might say years later. It was devastating then, but if he hadn't fired me, I'd still be stuck in that dead-end job and would never have discovered my true vocation as I was forced to do. Or we might say, Thank God so-and-so jilted me for someone else. At the time I felt it was a terrible betrayal, but the truth is, ours was a destructive, abusive relationship, and I might still be stuck in it if she hadn't done what she did. And I would never have met the love of my life whom I subsequently married. So sometimes this idea of *yisurin shel ahavah,* afflictions given out of love, seems to stand for the simple and verifiable idea that we don't always understand the events of our life properly; that often things we identify as calamities turn out to be blessings in disguise.

But at times the rabbis of the Talmud seem to discern something a bit darker in this idea. Drawing questionable support from an ambiguous line in the book of Psalms, Rabbi Huna says that when God loves a person, God crushes him or her with painful suffering. A truly horrifying idea, is it not? But we are still bound to ask, as we promised to do in every case, Is it ever true? Does God ever use suffering as an expression of love, a form of intimacy? Whenever I read this passage in the Talmud, I think of my colleague Rabbi Gerald Wolpe, whose wife was stricken with a debilitating stroke. Eventually she recovered most of what was lost, but it took a long time, and for many months she hovered on the brink of total incapacity. She could neither speak nor move, and it wasn't clear what, if anything, was going on in her mind. During these months, Rabbi Wolpe delivered one of the most powerful talks I have ever heard to a convention full of his rabbinic colleagues. "Before my wife's stroke," he began, "I only had a professional relationship with God." God was just an idea to him, something he was paid to talk about and explain. Now, of course, God was an intimate reality, a part of his moment-by-moment experience. Every second of his life now, he questioned God, accused God, poured out his rage at God, turned to God for consolation and deliverance. His wife's stroke had drawn Gerald Wolpe into an intimate embrace with God, and as painful as that bear hug may have been, it gave him an immediate and constant sense of the presence of God in his life.

But Rabbi Huna goes on, invoking a doctrine that would seem very much at home among the New Age theologies of current-day California. You might think, Rabbi Huna begins, that painful suffering could be seen as a sign of God's love even if the person upon whom it is visited doesn't accept it with love, but you would be wrong. Suffering given out of love only becomes so if it is accepted in love. So what Rabbi Huna is saying here is that our attitude actually changes the nature of reality. If we accept suffering with love, it becomes suffering given out of love. If we don't, it doesn't. It's just suffering. And again we must ask, Is this ever true?

It is certainly true that life comes at us in a chaotic torrent of data, and that we participate actively in giving shape and sense to the chaos. We tell ourselves a certain story, and data consistent with the story collects around it like iron filings around a magnet, while data not consistent with the story simply falls away unnoticed. So it is that we help to shape our own reality, to give it meaning and form. So it is that our attitude really does alter the nature of our reality.

A colleague told me about a woman in his congregation who died recently, leaving behind her an ethical will, a long, warmhearted testimony as to what the meaning of her life had been. The document was a study in gratitude. This was an extremely grateful woman. She wrote about how blessed and fortunate she was to have lived the life she had lived. She was grateful for her parents and her brothers, for their closeness during her childhood, and for the fact that neither the passage of time nor the considerable geographical distances between them ever diminished the sense of love and affection they felt for one another. She felt fortunate, too, to have had such loving relationships with her sisters-in-law, and to have had the pleasure of watching her nieces and nephews grow up so well.

She felt lucky to have had a cousin from Europe who became an intimate part of her family. He had come to live with them after the Holocaust. He and his wife had become a brother and sister to her, and their children were like nieces and nephews.

She wrote about how fortunate she had been to have had such good friends, the warmth, the love, and the caring of such a wide variety of people. She treasured the memory of all the *simchas*, the joyous occasions they had celebrated together, the trips they had taken together, the laughter and tears they had shared. But she had really hit the jackpot when it came to finding a husband. Maybe she was just too naive or complacent, she said, but she could not recall a single moment in her adult life when she had wanted to trade places with another woman. Her husband was one of a kind, she said, and she was lucky to have had him. And she was extremely grateful for his loyalty and help during the difficult months of her final illness. She went on in a similar vein about her children and her grandchildren, and the doctors and nurses and hospice attendants who had cared for her in the last months of her life.

My colleague's first thought upon reading this document was, "Is this woman kidding herself?" Many people do, of course. They claim to have perfect lives, perfect spouses and children —

their son is at Yale and their daughter at Harvard, and their husband is loving, thoughtful, considerate, *and* rich. But then we get to know them, and when we begin to scratch below the surface of their lives, we encounter the same dysfunctional mess we find in most families we know. But my colleague knew this woman, and she never struck him as a person who was kidding herself. She always seemed for real to him.

So what then? Was she just lucky? Did she just happen to have great parents and siblings, terrific friends, the perfect husband, and children other people could only dream of having? My colleague knew them too, and this certainly wasn't the case. Her friends and family were just like everybody else. There was nothing extraordinary about them. They were profoundly mixed human beings, fundamentally good people with the full human complement of foibles and flaws.

The one who was extraordinary was her. She was a woman with an exceptional capacity for gratitude. When we treat people as a blessing, they usually respond in kind. When we are grateful for the people in our lives, they often become people worthy of the gratitude we feel for them. This had been this woman's secret: she had made everyone around her into wonderful people by her gift for appreciating them. Her capacity for gratitude had created a beautiful reality in her life. It had made ordinary people extraordinary; it had made the commonplace sacred. Her attitude had changed the nature of her life. This, I think, is the kind of thing the rabbis had in mind when they suggested that *yisurin shel ahavah* — afflictions given out of love — become so only if accepted with love. Our attitude — in this case, a kind of gratitude for what we have been given — shapes our reality, changes the meaning of what happens to us, turns ordinary people into extraordinary people and apparently purposeless suffering into suffering given out of love.

The rabbis truly love this idea. They had devoted only a few sentences to the first two propositions, but they go on and on for pages about *yisurin shel ahavah,* considering it from many theological vantage points. Could an affliction be considered *yisurin shel ahavah* if it prevented you from praying or studying Torah? The rabbis decide that the answer in both cases is no, and then they observe that the three greatest gifts God had ever given Israel — the Torah, the land of Israel, and the World to Come — were each given through great suffering, a classic demonstration of the doctrine. It is an invaluable idea to them because it enables them to imagine that there is an explanation for suffering; it is something they can understand and therefore control. Even if they don't understand an affliction when it comes upon them, if it isn't a consequence of something they have done or of their general impiety, they can assume that it must be a case of *yisurin shel ahavah.*

But then Rabbi Yochanan pipes up and spoils the whole party by uttering a single word — *banim* (children). This was a code word, and all the rabbis understood what it meant. It was rabbinic shorthand for the premature death of one's own children, and with this single word Rabbi Yochanan had raised a truly terrifying possibility that his own experience had forced him to acknowledge. Could it be that there was such a thing as irredeemable suffering; suffering with no saving qualities; meaningless suffering? Rabbi Yochanan had lost ten children himself — in fact he wore the bone of the tenth child he had lost around his neck — and he knew as well as anyone that there was no consequence that could ever move us to say that the death of a child had been worth it, a blessing in disguise, an example of *yisurin shel ahavah.* There was suffering that could not be controlled, that could not be submitted to the intellect's rage to order and pacify our experience.

The rabbis mount a vigorous defense against Yochanan's assertion, but they cannot ward him off. His argument is unassailable. Whenever they knock it down, it pops right back up again.

Then suddenly the argument stops altogether, and without either introduction or context the Talmud tells a triptych of stories, or one story, actually, told three times. In the first telling Rabbi Hiyya Bar Abba falls deathly ill and Rabbi Yochanan comes to comfort him. "Are your sufferings beloved to you?" Rabbi Yochanan asks. He seems here to be invoking the doctrine of *yisurin shel ahavah,* and particularly the idea that if we receive our suffering in love, it will become a suffering given out of love — a suffering with a reward in the end. But Rabbi Hiyya seems annoyed at this intrusion of theological correctness in the midst of his suffering. "Neither my sufferings nor any reward I might receive for them are beloved to me," Hiyya replies. "Give me your hand, then," Rabbi Yochanan says, and Rabbi Hiyya gives him his hand and he heals him.

What is the point of this story? Rashi and other commentators simply saw it as an example of Rabbi Yochanan's magical healing powers. Such powers were commonplace among the rabbis of the Talmud. Jesus wasn't the only figure of the rabbinic age who was regarded as a faith healer. But other commentators see a more complex meaning in this story. When Rabbi Hiyya dismisses Rabbi Yochanan's question so abruptly, he seems to awaken Yochanan to the futility of theology in the face of suffering. What does seem to work in such circumstances? Empathy, the human touch, the presence of another: "He said give me your hand. He gave him his hand and he healed him."

I became sensitized to the considerable healing power of simply being present after being thrust many times into situations where I had little else to offer. In my work as both a chaplain and a congregational rabbi, I have often been called upon to tend to people who are in comas or who are otherwise less than fully conscious. At first I hated this kind of work. I would feel impotent, frustrated, and would often say a quick prayer and then flee the room as quickly as possible. Finally, for lack of an alternative, I decided to pay attention to what I was doing. After sitting in silence by the side of people in comas for long periods of time, I began to become aware of very subtle signs of consciousness and communication: the pattern of breathing and how it changed, involuntary sighing and what brought it on, the sudden movement of a hand or a finger. But beyond these things, I became aware of the ineffable sense of a presence in the room. We often take this sense for granted when a loved one enters a room we are in. They may be behind us, and perhaps they don't make a sound when they come in, but still we know they are there. We can feel them. We are touched by their presence, their being. Often I will enter the room of a person in a coma in a state of some agitation myself. Perhaps I will have come from a particularly hectic day, and the reverberations of all the activities and complications I have been experiencing will still be ringing in my psyche. But as I sit in stillness by the bedside of this person, I will begin to come to myself; I will begin to feel a sense of my own being, my own presence, the radiant stillness of my own awareness underneath all the agitation I have experienced that day. And no sooner do I begin to experience this than I also feel another consciousness, another presence in the room — the presence of the comatose patient I am visiting. This is the most profound form of human contact there is. More than once, people have awakened from their comas to tell me that they remembered being with me, having contact with me this way while they were unconscious. Experiences like these taught me that it is precisely this naked sense of being with, being in contact, being to being, that is at the bottom of all healing exchanges. Even when we are speaking to people, this primary, nonverbal exchange is going on beneath the surface of what we are saying, and it is this exchange which is really significant, truly healing.

The second telling of the story is identical to the first, word for word, only this time it is Rabbi Yochanan who falls deathly ill and Rabbi Hanina who comes to comfort him. There is a post-script to the story this time, a question the rabbis ask about it. Since in the first story Rabbi Yochanan healed Rabbi Hiyya by touching him, why doesn't he just heal himself now? The Talmud answers its own question. "The prisoner cannot free himself from prison," the Talmud says.

What does this mean? What does it add to our understanding of the first telling of this story? For one thing, it seems to emphasize that the critical element in healing is the presence of another human being. We cannot heal ourselves with our own presence. It is the presence of someone else — a presence beyond our own — that makes it work. The prison in the rabbis' metaphor is the prison of the self, the ego. And in fact the feeling of isolation and alienation, of being imprisoned in our aloneness, is often exaggerated by serious illness, an ordeal that places us squarely in another world from the people we know. This is why Paul Cowan, writing in the *Village Voice* in the mid-1980s, entitled his account of his own terminal illness "In Another Country." When we are threatened with death, consciously struggling for life, our concerns are necessarily different from the concerns of the people we know. We live in another country.

I was very struck by this phenomenon when I was working as a chaplain at Memorial Sloane-Kettering Hospital in New York. People would lie in bed struggling with the grim reaper all day long and their friends would come in on weekends and holidays dressed in their glad rags, in party clothes and beach attire. It was as if they had come from another world. People threatened with terminal illnesses have an irresistible need to tie up the loose ends of their lives — to pay off their bills, to balance their checkbooks, to see that their funeral arrangements are all in order. But their relatives have very different needs, and chief among them is the need to preserve their denial of death. Consequently they often see these concerns as morbid and defeatist. "Don't talk to me about funeral arrangements," they will say. "You're not going to die." The sense of incongruity, of isolation, of people trapped in parallel but unconnected universes becomes acute. Another human presence attuned to our predicament frees us from this prison, opens us to the awareness that our consciousness is not discrete, that it is not as hemmed in by the limits of the self as we might have imagined, and that therefore we are not bound. And this is in fact a great healing, particularly at a time when our greatest fear might be that our consciousness is about to be annihilated, that we are about to become nothing. The felt sharing of another human presence encourages us to imagine that our awareness is not really *ours* after all, but rather something we share, a part of a larger awareness that will continue beyond us whether or not we endure as separate selves. It is the prison of our individuality that the presence of another frees us from.

This is why I always offer prayers in Hebrew to people I am visiting in the hospital, even when they assure me that they are not the least bit religious. Occasionally — very rarely, actually — they will politely decline the offer. They will say, "No thank you, Rabbi. I've made it this far without religion, and I'd prefer to keep it that way." Most of the time they will make a joke out of it. They will say, "Why not? Any port in a storm! Might as well cover all the bases." But when the prayer starts, and they hear the ancient Hebrew intoned, more often than not they are profoundly moved, often to tears. I am convinced that this is because the ancient Hebrew connects them to a spiritual consciousness larger than their own, a community of meaning that will continue long after their own life has ceased. The prayers release them from the bounds of the self.

The third telling of the story repeats elements of the first two but is quite a bit fuller. It emerges from the first two as a difficult truth might slowly emerge from a patient in therapy, or as a lover might haltingly confess to an infidelity, the truth finally standing naked after several sputtering attempts to get it out.

As it begins, Rabbi Eleazar has fallen deathly ill and Rabbi Yochanan has come to visit him. Upon entering the room, Rabbi Yochanan observes that it is dark, so he rolls up his sleeve and lights up the room with the radiance of the skin on his arm. (Rashi's idea that Rabbi Yochanan was a charismatic faith healer cannot be completely dismissed after all, I suppose.) With the room so lit, Yochanan sees that Rabbi Eleazar is weeping. "Why are you weeping?" he asks. And then he proceeds to violate every principle of pastoral counseling. First of all, he doesn't even wait for an answer to his own question. Rather, he blunders ahead with his own theories as to why Rabbi Eleazar is weeping. Is it because Rabbi Eleazar hasn't learned enough Torah? Well, that doesn't matter, Rabbi Yochanan reassures him. After all, it matters not if we learn much or if we learn little, as long as our hearts are directed toward heaven.

The Talmud records no response from Rabbi Eleazar, but Rabbi Yochanan blunders on. "Are you weeping because you have lacked sustenance during your life? This shouldn't bother you either. After all, not everyone merits two tables." (Learning and wealth, or perhaps this world and the next, Rashi theorizes. In other words, Eleazar, a great scholar, has had Torah. That should have been enough for him. He shouldn't be greedy and think that he should have had wealth as well.)

Again no answer from Rabbi Eleazar is recorded, and Rabbi Yochanan forges ahead: Is it because of children? Once more that code word: Rabbi Yochanan means now, as he did earlier, the loss of children — the premature death of one's child. Like Rabbi Yochanan, Rabbi Eleazar has also suffered this most difficult of all losses. And here is where Rabbi Yochanan really flunks out of chaplaincy school. "Are you weeping because of the loss of your children? Well, this is the bone of my tenth son," he says. As we mentioned earlier, Rabbi Yochanan had lost ten children, and he wore the bone of his tenth son around his neck. Now he holds up the bone to Rabbi Eleazar as if to say, You think you've got it bad? I've lost ten children, so what are you complaining about? This, of course, is the worst thing we can possibly say to someone we are counseling for suffering. We need to acknowledge their suffering and not belittle it. We must give it credence, not dismiss it or compare it unfavorably to our own.

Finally Rabbi Eleazar speaks up. It is almost as if he can't bear to hear any more from Rabbi Yochanan. "This is why I am weeping," he says. "I am weeping for *cal hai shufra d'balei b'afra* — I am weeping for all this perfection, all this beauty which is fading into the earth."

What does this answer mean? Rashi, always focused on the personal radiance of Rabbi Yochanan, thinks it is a statement of regret concerning this worthy. Rabbi Eleazar is weeping because his own impending death reminds him that the beautiful Rabbi Yochanan will also someday die. But Rabbi Joseph Soleveitchik, one of the seminal figures in the American Modern Orthodox movement, sees something much more profound in Rabbi Eleazar's words. According to Rabbi Soleveitchik, there are two kinds of suffering in this world. The first he calls relative suffering. I stubbed my toe and my foot hurts. My wife has left me and I am bereft. I have just learned that I have cancer and I am frightened to death. But even when things are going well for us, when our toe does not hurt, and our wife is safe and happy at home, even when we are in perfect health, we nevertheless experience a baseline of suffering, which Soleveitchik calls absolute suffering. Absolute suffering, he says, flows from the fact that we live in a perfect world, a world of radiance and beauty, but we are unable to see it as such until it is slipping from our grasp. Only then can we apprehend its perfection, and as soon as we do, we are struck by the tragic understanding that all this perfection is impermanent, fading into the earth, gone as soon as we glimpse it.

For Rabbi Soleveitchik the common experience of nostalgia is an example of absolute suffering. When we think of those days long ago in another city, they seem perfect to us. They seem vivid and beautiful in a way our lives do not seem now. We remember that they did not seem that way to us then either, so we assume that this nostalgic feeling is just an illusion, a trick the mind plays on us. But no, Rabbi Soleveitchik insists, it is not an illusion. Our lives really were that perfect, that vivid back then. It's just that we are only capable of experiencing this perfection after it is gone, after it has faded. It was for this reason that Rabbi Eleazar was weeping. He was fading into the earth himself, and he was finally seeing the world in its true state, in its true perfection.

I am convinced that Rabbi Soleveitchik was right. I once saw such tears myself, and it was exactly as he explained it. It happened when I was working as a hospice chaplain at Beth Israel Hospital in New York. There was a patient named Maury who had more rabbis tending to him than anyone I have ever met. He had grown up in a synagogue in Brooklyn, and that rabbi was now looking after him. He had helped to found a synagogue in Manhattan, then became disenchanted, broke away, and founded another synagogue right down the street, and the rabbis from both these synagogues were now tending to him as well. His brother-in-law was a prominent rabbi from Chicago. And now Maury had joined the hospice, so I was in on his case as well. This guy was positively lousy with rabbis. Every time I went to visit him, I had to stand on a line of rabbis before I could get in to see him.

But none of us was doing him much good. Maury was having a very difficult approach to death. He was terribly fearful, in a full-on panic a good deal of the time. Although he was really dying from a virulent cancer, every day he imagined that he was dying from something else and had himself rushed to every emergency ward in the city. The emergency room doctors were losing patience with him. Once I had to go and retrieve him from the emergency room at Columbia Presbyterian. The doctors there had become so frustrated with him that they had put him out on the street in his stocking feet in the middle of a snowstorm. I hailed a cab for him and wrapped his frozen feet in my scarf as we rode.

But he really was dying. I had to keep reminding myself of that. And one day he had himself taken to the emergency room at Roosevelt Hospital, where he slipped into what everyone assumed would be his final coma. I stopped by Roosevelt every morning on my way to work to sit with him for a while. But on the fourth day, I could see as I came in that he was sitting up in bed. I was shocked. None of his doctors had expected him to come out of this coma. And as I got closer to his bed, I could see that there was something very strange about him. He seemed to be soaking wet. His bed-clothes were completely soaked. It was almost as if someone had hosed him down. It wasn't until I got to his bedside that I realized what was going on. He was weeping profusely, and he was completely covered in tears.

"Maury, what's wrong? Why are you weeping?" I said.

"Rabbi," he said, "four days ago I felt myself slipping into what I was sure would be my final coma. But then this morning I woke up, and now look at this!" With that, Maury swept his arm across the wardroom like a magic wand, and something about his gesture allowed me to see precisely what he was seeing. We were in one of those big old hospital wards at Roosevelt, the kind with ten or twelve beds and big vaulting windows. An immense shaft of sunlight was beaming in through one of those windows, and there were dust motes swirling around in the sunbeam like spiral nebulae. Nurses glided noiselessly around the ward like angels. We were in a perfect, radiant world.

Maury held my hand in an iron grip. "This is religion," he said. And I suppose what he meant in part was that all that business with the rabbis who were standing in line to see him was not. But what I was thinking was, "This is the weeping of Rabbi Eleazar." This is that last glimpse of the perfection of this world we get just before it fades away from us. In fact Maury died a fearless death a few hours later.

So I have reason to believe that Rabbi Soleveitchik was correct. When Rabbi Eleazar says that he is weeping because of all this perfection that is fading into the earth, he is saying, Look, all you rabbis have been asking the wrong question all along. You have been asking about relative suffering. Why do we suffer? We suffer because we suffer. We suffer because suffering is endemic to our experience. Suffering is one of the deepwater mysteries of human existence. It can neither be explained nor controlled, but it can be met by a deepwater mystery of equal force — the mystery of human presence. As the story continues, Rabbi Yochanan utterly redeems himself. "Well, if that's what you're weeping about," he says, "well, of course you should weep." And the two of them then weep together.

Strangely enough, this third telling of the story ends just as the other two did. "Are your sufferings beloved to you?" Rabbi Yochanan asks. "Neither my sufferings nor any reward I might receive for them are beloved to me," Rabbi Eleazar replies. The theological litmus test is utterly transformed here. Now it reads like a joke of infinite poignancy which Yochanan and Eleazar share with a heartbreaking tenderness. They are both fully in on this joke, and the healing that follows is now utterly believable. "Give me your hand, then," Rabbi Yochanan says, and Rabbi Eleazar gives him his hand and he heals him. We can feel the healing power of the compassionate presence that passes between them. Suffering is suffering. It can neither be controlled nor explained, but we can meet it with compassion, with presence.

As if this truth is too frightening to bear, as if they have come a little too close to the fire and have burned themselves a bit, the rabbis of the Talmud now seem to recoil, to back off from this beautiful but frightening truth they have uncovered. They now tell a fourth story, a simple, unvarnished magical tale of reward and punishment. A hundred jugs of wine belonging to Rav Huna suddenly go bad and turn into vinegar. The rabbis come to see him and they tell him, "Master, you had better examine your behavior." It turns out that he hadn't been giving his tenant the proper share of his vine twigs. He promises to redress this inequity, and as a consequence, some say, the vinegar immediately turned into wine again, while others say that the price of vinegar suddenly went up until it sold for the same price as wine.

Wouldn't it be pretty to think so, as Jake Barnes asked at the end of *The Sun Also Rises*. Pretty perhaps, but not beautiful, not perfect. Only the truth is beautiful. Only the truth is perfect, and the truth is almost always frightening. The truth can never be explained nor controlled, and we often enter it through the gateway of our suffering, a portal of fire we are disinclined to enter. Meditation can help us overcome this disinclination. Meditation is a resolute being with whatever we experience, a path to the depths of our own presence, and to that even deeper sense of being we share with others. At the end of the Garden of Eden story, the Torah tells us that angels bearing fiery swords are stationed at the four gates of the garden. In meditation we learn that these fiery swords are not meant to keep us out of paradise, but rather to vault us in.

PRACTICE POINTS

Being With and Turning Toward Afflictive States

Anger, anxiety, boredom, depression, frustration, meaninglessness — these are states of mind we all experience. But we don't like them, and our first unconscious instinct is to turn away from them, to deny them, to try to change our circumstances so they will go away. Or else we spasm on them — freeze them in our minds by fixating on them instead of allowing them to simply rise up and then fall away again as they are naturally inclined to do. In this way we allow them to become the headwaters for a long meandering stream of afflictive thoughts with many torturous tributaries. But what if we turned toward these states instead? What if we allowed ourselves to inhabit them, to feel them as fully as we could? Doing so might release the considerable energy these states contain and make this energy available to us. Doing so might free us from the sense that these states of mind are afflicting us in the first place. Filling them up with our consciousness, we might find ourselves coming out the other side into a wider, less constricted space.

In order for any of this to happen, we first have to become fully aware of these states, to break ourselves of the habit of pushing them away. A good place to start working on breaking this habit is the mild (or sometimes not so mild) physical pain we might experience in the course of sitting meditation. Perhaps our knees begin to ache as we sit. Perhaps our back hurts. Perhaps our foot falls asleep. Our first instinct is to move our legs, to change our position so that the pain goes away. Or perhaps we decide to just sit there and let the pain lead us on a long and detailed contemplation of precisely how long we might be expected to endure this pain, how it compares to other pain we have felt, whether or not it is genuinely life threatening, et cetera. Perhaps we might spend our time in meditation clenching every muscle in our body and holding on against this pain for dear life until the bell rings, putting us out of our misery. These are all attempts to push the pain away, to get rid of it somehow, either by changing our circumstances so that it doesn't appear to exist anymore, or by covering it over with a mind full of screamingly painful thoughts.

But what if we were to *become* the pain in our legs, to inhabit it, to turn toward it as completely as we could? Then, I think, we might not experience it as pain anymore, but rather as simple sensation. We would be aware that these impulses were emanating up from our legs in waves, but they wouldn't necessarily hurt us. Pain is often the differential between how we want things to be and how they actually are. Pushing pain away indicates that we wish it were somehow otherwise. Turning toward it, being with it, on the other hand, releases us from the pain of it. No longer wishing it to be otherwise, we can enjoy it for what it is, namely pure sensation, pure energy, a momentary impulse-wave. It is enjoyable, it is gratifying, to experience a strong sensation. We feel more fully alive when we do; our life seems more vivid.

Once we are able to transform the simple physical pain we experience in meditation this way, we may wish to move on to the more diffuse and even more painful world of afflictive emotional states such as anger, anxiety, and boredom. When anger arises in our mind, either in meditation or when we are walking down the street, we might accustom ourselves to turning toward it, embracing it, experiencing it to the fullest extent possible, rather than turning away from it, trying to control it in some way, or worst of all, acting on it. Our usual response to afflictive emotional states such as anger and anxiety is either to deny them, to express them inappropriately, or to tell ourselves self-justifying stories about them. The first response, denial, causes serious inner damage; the second, inappropriate acting out, sets off a whole new chain of afflictive states of its own; the third, creating a drama complete with villains on whom we can place the blame, augments and perpetuates the disturbance. But there is another way. Getting into the habit of embracing our pain can be the first step toward getting past it by moving from the melodrama of suffering and affliction to a more pleasurable and primary world of impulse, energy, and sensation.

Visiting the Sick and the Art of Simply Being Present

Bikur cholim, visiting the sick, is one of the fundamental Jewish expressions of *gemilut chesed* (loving-kindness), but it is also a great vehicle for spiritual practice. In ten years of Zen meditation, I learned to cultivate a deep sense of simply being present. Moving from this practice to an observant Jewish life, I found that *bikur cholim*, above all other Jewish practices, was the one that required me to call upon this sense most insistently.

Every time I stand outside a hospital room before a visit, I go through a moment of meditation at the threshold. I stand still there, taking stock of my state of mind; invariably it includes at least a touch of fear. I am frightened because, deep down, I feel responsible for saving the person who is ill, and of course I cannot. I cannot make them well nor save them from death, if that is where their illness seems to be taking them. So there at the threshold, I remind myself that I have not come to *do* anything at all, but simply to be with the person I am visiting. Simple human presence is the greatest gift we can convey to anyone, no matter what their state of health, but this truth is particularly evident when we visit the sick.

Sometimes, in fact, there are things that we *can* do for someone who is ill. We can bring them the telephone when it rings, or wipe their brow, or call the nurse for them if they need her. We can listen to them; their illness may have touched a deep chord in their psyche, may have set off a considerable disturbance there, and there may be quite a bit they need to get off their chest. Sometimes our presence can be comforting because it relieves them of their loneliness. Sometimes it can even bring a sense of meaning to their predicament. Their illness may well have shattered the beliefs from which they derived purpose in their lives, but they may find it quite meaningful that you care about them, that you have taken the trouble to come. Or when you pray for them in the language and customs of a particular religious culture, they may find it comforting to be connected to a community of meaning larger than their own, one that will go on even after their own life has come to an end.

But most of this comes under the category of simply being present anyway, being present to bring them the phone, to listen, to relieve them of their sense of isolation. So making bikur cholim a part of your spiritual practice, and pausing at the doorway to engage in this sort of meditation when you do, can be quite beneficial, quite helpful in your own attempt to cultivate a strong sense of simply being present. The more immediate and vivid your sense of your own presence is, of course, the more you will have to bring to this encounter, and meditation is certainly one way to deepen and expand this sense.

Often the most difficult step in practicing bikur cholim is just getting started. To visit the sick and the dying is to put ourselves in the presence of suffering, when our usual instinct is to avoid it. So there is a certain resistance we need to overcome, even when visiting friends and relatives who are ill. There is intimidation as well, that fear of not knowing what to do we spoke of earlier. But the good news is that there are increasing opportunities to practice bikur cholim in many American cities these days, and most of them involve some training to help get you over the intimidation barrier.

A growing number of synagogues have formed bikur cholim committees in recent years, having come to understand that the rabbis need not monopolize this practice the way they have for so long. In the traditional Jewish community, bikur cholim was seen as a communal obligation, a spiritual practice engaged in by everyone, not just the rabbi, and we are slowly but surely beginning to see the wisdom of this point of view. Most of these synagogue committees offer training in bikur cholim as well as regular opportunities to practice it. A new kind of institution, the Jewish healing center, has begun to emerge in recent years in New York, San Francisco, and other major American cities. These centers also offer training in bikur cholim and tend to be particularly sensitive to the spiritual opportunities it presents. Finally there is hospice. All hospice programs, Jewish and otherwise, depend heavily on the participation of volunteers and offer fairly extensive volunteer training in how to care for the dying. The opportunities for cultivating the practice of visiting the sick and the dying are increasingly available for anyone who is sincerely interested in doing so.

Chapter Three

The Inner Roots of Conflict

1. Forward from Eden

THE TRUTH OFTEN COMES IN THREES. THERE IS ANOTHER triptych in the Torah that has a great deal to teach us about one of the most common forms of suffering, interpersonal conflict. The three stories are three of the earliest narratives the Torah tells us: the story of Adam and Eve's expulsion from the Garden of Eden; the story of the conflict between Cain and Abel; and the story of the Tower of Babel.

In the first of these stories, Adam is placed in the Garden of Eden and is told by God, "Of every tree in the garden, you may freely eat, but of the Tree of the Knowledge of Good and Evil, you may not eat." Eve is created out of Adam's rib to be a companion and a helpmeet, but she doesn't appear to be all that helpful at first. The serpent goes to work on her right away. He tells her she will not, in fact, die if she eats the forbidden fruit. Instead her eyes will open, and she will be like a god, knowing good from evil as only gods do. Eve's desire for this fruit and for the godly wisdom it will bring her becomes inflamed, and she eats the fruit and gives some to Adam, who also eats it without hesitation.

We can infer a number of things from Adam's behavior. First of all, his desire for the fruit must have been as strong as hers, even if it was unexpressed. Otherwise why would he eat it without a word of protest? This would not be the last marriage in which the wife expressed an impulse she and her husband shared but only she was able to express. Nor would it be the last marriage in which the partners divvied up their ambivalence. I have seen this in the course of marital counseling hundreds of times. A husband and wife take the two extremes of an argument while married. They break up (often because of this very disagreement), and then both of them move quickly back to the center of the argument, to the place of an ambivalence they both secretly shared all along. Now it becomes clear: the husband has been tacitly assigned to one pole and the wife to the other, but the truth is they are both in conflict, both confused as to what they want. Before the divorce, he said he wanted to live like a beatnik, and she said she wanted to be rich. They get divorced, and then they both live a middle-class life tinged with bohemianism. Adam and Eve are both ambivalent here. They both know the fruit is forbidden, and they both want it. Eve has been assigned to express the polarity of desire, but it's clear from how quickly Adam eats the fruit, from the complete absence of any demur on his part, that he wants it as much as she does.

In any case, they eat the fruit and their eyes are opened, just as the snake predicted, but it is not pleasant for either of them. Their innocent, undifferentiated experience of the world gives way to a harsh dualism; the world is now divided between good and evil, pleasure and pain. They become conscious of their nakedness and take fig leaves to cover it. Hearing the voice of God in the garden, they feel guilty and try to hide among the trees. God calls out to Adam, "Ayecah?" — "Where are you?" This is an existential rather than a geographical question, and it provokes an existential answer. "I was afraid because I was naked so I hid," Adam replies. "How did you know you were naked?" God demands to know, and Adam, still given to hiding, promptly blames everything on Eve, who in turn blames everything on the snake. God will have none of it and punishes all three. The snake will henceforth have to crawl on its belly. Eve is doomed to bear children in pain and is made dependent on her husband for the gratification of her desires. Adam, who used to enjoy the fruits of the earth at his leisure, will now have to work for a living, to till the dust he is made of until he returns to it. So it is that childbirth, work, and death, all previously unknown, suddenly burst into existence. God says, "Behold, this man has become as one of us, knowing good and evil." We better get him out of the garden before he eats from the Tree of Life and lives forever! So Adam is driven out of the garden, and cherubim with a fiery sword that turns in every direction are stationed east of Eden to guard the way to the Tree of Life.

This is the story of an inner conflict. Adam and Eve are struggling with themselves, with the mysterious urge to have the one thing they are forbidden to have. Even in paradise, it seems, we were afflicted with the desire to have things be somehow otherwise, an impulse which, then as now, brings about our undoing, suffering and death. Then as now, we were afflicted by a powerful tendency to deny our responsibility for all this. After they eat the forbidden fruit, Adam and Eve first try to hide from God, and then, after God finds them and confronts them directly, they blame each other for their predicament.

The second story, the story of Cain and Abel, arises directly out of the first. Denied and sublimated, Adam and Eve's inner conflict bursts to the surface again in the form of a struggle between their two sons. This, I think, is why the Torah takes pains to tell us that Adam and Eve conceive Cain and then Abel immediately upon their expulsion from the garden. The first story gives birth to the second. Cain, a farmer, makes an offering to God from the fruits of the land. Abel, a shepherd, also brings an offering, but his is from the first and best and fattest of his flocks. Abel's offering is accepted but Cain's is not. God makes it clear that Cain himself is responsible for this rejection. "Why be angry?" God says to Cain. "Why let your face fall? If you do your best, you'll be lifted up, but if you don't do your best, sin crouches at the door, and it wants you — it has a strong urge for you. But you can rule over it. You can control it." Nevertheless, Cain does not. The call to responsibility is wasted on Cain, who, like his parents, prefers to deny his complicity in his own unhappiness. He would rather blame his brother. He cannot resist the temptation to exorcise his own failure by projecting it onto Abel in the form of jealousy, so he goes out to the fields and kills Abel straightaway.

This is a starkly familiar story, is it not? Someone else is chosen over us — for a job, by a lover — and the last thing we want to do is to consider the possibility that they should have been chosen, that they deserved to be. How much easier it is to let ourselves fall into the grip of resentment or jealousy — even of loved ones and friends — an antipathy so strong we become willing to destroy the closest of relationships.

"Where is Abel your brother?" God asks. Again this is not a geographical question. "Am I my brother's keeper?" Cain replies. "Your brother's blood cries to me from the earth," God says, and then he pronounces Cain's punishment. The earth, which opened its mouth to drink in Abel's blood from Cain's hand, will no longer yield its strength to Cain, no matter how hard he works it. He will become a fugitive and a wanderer on the earth. He goes out from the presence of God and lives in Nod, east of Eden. In addition to death and exile, which came into the world as a consequence of the first story, we now have failure and jealousy as well.

Now Cain and his wife conceive children. Many generations of grotesque, brutal creatures ensue, and the world becomes awash with violence. Then, after the earth is cleansed by a great flood (it seems likely that the entire flood narrative is a late insertion), we get the third story of our triptych. All of humanity, we are told, is of one language, one speech. We journey eastward and settle on a plain in the land of Shinar. There we make a great breakthrough: we discover the technology of firing bricks. Infatuated with ourselves, we imagine ourselves to be all-powerful. "Come, let us build a city," we say, "with its top in heaven. Let's make a name for ourselves, so we don't get scattered over the face of the earth." Let's build a city, we say, the work of our own hands, the assertion of our own will, in which the will of God, so apparent in nature, is obscured. Let's use our newfound power to build an artifice in which our own will can supplant the will of God, so that we are no longer subject to that will — God will no longer have the power to scatter us wherever he pleases.

Again, a not unfamiliar story in a world where we worship our technologies and imagine they have made us all-powerful; a world in which we have built urban environments that we imagine have made us immune to the laws of nature; a world in which we believe that if we shut our eyes tightly enough, we can pursue our own will, our greed and our fear, all the way to heaven without suffering any consequences at all.

Using our new bricks and the simple slime of the earth for mortar, we begin to raise up the towers of our new city, but God does not approve. "Behold! They are one people, and they have one language, and this is what they begin to do! Now no purpose of theirs can be withheld from them," God observes in evident horror. I have given them the earth and they want heaven too. I have given them a harmonious world that works according to my will, but they want to supplant that will with their own. I have given them what is, but they want something else. "Come, let us go down and confuse their speech so they can't understand each other." God then scatters us across the face of the earth — exactly the fate we were trying to avoid — and the city is never completed.

The Torah takes some pains to connect these three stories both linguistically and thematically. In two of them (the Garden of Eden and the Tower of Babel stories) God, who is supposed to be One and therefore alone in the heavens, nevertheless addresses a mysterious other or others up there. "Behold, this man has become as one of us, knowing good and evil," God laments just before the expulsion from Eden. And at Babel, when God sees humanity proposing to build a tower that will reach all the way to heaven, he says, "Come, let us go down and confuse their speech." Two of the stories (the Garden of Eden and the Cain and Abel stories) feature versions of the same rhetorical question — "*Ayecah?*" ("Where are you?") in the first instance, and "*Eih Hevel achichah?*" ("Where is Abel your brother?") in the second. God knows very well where Adam is in the first instance and where Abel is in the second. These questions are designed to provoke both Adam and Cain to inquire as to their spiritual rather than their geographical locations. And they are designed to connect the two stories as well, to reinforce the idea that the second comes out of the first.

But the clearest connection between these three stories is the fact that each of them is introduced and/or concluded by some form of the word *kedem*. The Garden of Eden story is introduced with the phrase "And God planted a garden in Eden *mi-kedem*" (usually translated here as "eastward"), and at the end of this story we read, "And he drove out the man and *mi-kedem* [at the east of] the garden" he placed the cherubim with the flaming sword. . . . This line pivots us into the Cain and Abel story, which ends with the line "And Cain went out from the presence of God and dwelt in the land of Nod, *kedmat eden* [east of Eden]." Finally, the Tower of Babel story is introduced by these words: "And it came to pass when they journeyed *mi-kedem* [from the east] . . ."

Although I have translated *kedem* and its derivative *mi-kedem* as "east" or "eastward" or "from the east" here, the word is really a lot more complicated than that. Hebrew is a pre-dualistic language, and *kedem* is one of many Hebrew words that expresses both itself and its opposite. *Kedem* is a temporal marker, but it carries us beyond our ordinary linear sense of time. It means to advance and to go forward, but it also means to go back in time. *Kedem* is both the east, the place where the sun rises and the day begins, and the ancient past, the days of old, the days that came first, at the very beginning of the march of time. As a verb it means "to advance." As a noun it means "the place of origin." *Kedem* is a two-way hinge, a word that goes backward and forward at once. Having the word *kedem* in common not only connects the three stories under discussion; it also suggests that they form a progression of sorts, that they are points on a time line, a continuum that goes two ways at once. All three stories are about conflict, and the progression seems to be one that moves from the inside out in increasingly widening spirals.

The conflict in the first story is between Adam (and Eve) and God. It is therefore an interior struggle, a kind of reformulation of the Second Noble Truth we enumerated earlier. Adam is in paradise. He has everything he needs, and everything is permitted to him except one thing — the fruit of the Tree of the Knowledge of Good and Evil. Yet this is the one thing he wants — that which he does not have, that which is external to him. This inner conflict drives the first story, but even after the expulsion from Eden, it seems to continue in sublimated form in the conflict between Cain and Abel.

Cain also wants what he does not have — God's approval. Rather than face his own failure, his own complicity in his disappointment, Cain projects it onto the person of his brother Abel and kills him. After this, violence and murder fill the world. A generation of brutes rises up, and the world is overrun by violent conflict. Conflict begins in our own heart, and then we project it onto others, and this kind of projection proliferates until the world is full of violence and conflict.

The Tower of Babel story completes the progression. Now all of humanity sets itself against the will of God. Now all of humanity rebels against the way things are, against the world they have been given, the way Adam did individually in the beginning.

We have been given the earth, but we want heaven too. We have been given a certain capacity to control ourselves, but we want to control everything. God seems threatened by these aspirations, as well he should be. Every time we go to war, we do so under the illusion that we can assert control over the world, but instead we invariably unleash a horrifying train of unanticipated consequences. Loosed from their restraints, human brutality and violence usually show a virulence and a depth we never quite manage to foresee — My Lai, Abu Ghraib — and set off a cycle of response far beyond our capacity to control. "Behold! They are one people, and they have one language, and this is what they begin to do!" God says to his mysterious unnamed companion at the Tower of Babel. And God makes a similar declaration at the Garden of Eden. "Behold, this man has become as one of us, knowing good and evil" — and now, let's get him out of here before he puts forth his hand and takes also of the Tree of Life.

Clearly there is something about man as an individual and humankind as a collective whole that is both more powerful and more threatening to God than we have imagined. We are made in the image of God and we are conscious of having been made this way. We were given a will of our own and the power of speech. Used blindly or unwisely, these powers seem to threaten existence itself. Perhaps this is what the great biblical scholar Yochanan Muffs meant when he said that the Bible is a tragedy and God is its tragic hero: heroic because he had the courage to make a creature with the power to threaten his own creation; tragic because this creature was constantly abusing this power and breaking God's heart. So we see God struggling with this power, which he himself must have been the source of, and we see Adam and Eve and Cain and the people of Babel struggling with it as well.

This struggle, which begins in the heart of a single person, ripples out until finally it has filled the heart of all humankind. The argument advances (*kadmah*) until it has returned to its source (*mi-kedem*); it is an argument between God and God's most prized creation, an internal argument, an internal struggle.

2. Deep Wells Covered Over by Conflict

After the Tower of Babel, the primal conflict continues in every generation, embodied now by the struggle between the elder and younger son for hegemony in the family. Isaac usurps his older brother Ishmael. Jacob overthrows Esau, Joseph supplants his ten older brothers. Moses becomes more powerful than Aaron, his older brother. David, the youngest and smallest of Jesse's ten sons, usurps not only his older brothers but the very tall and senior King Saul.

This dynamic is presented most directly in the story of Jacob and Esau, where it is portrayed as endemic to human life. It does not arise out of our experience; rather it begins in the womb. Jacob and Esau are in conflict from before they were born. Their striving against each other in Rebecca's belly is so disturbing to her that she cries out to God, "If this is how it's going to be, why should I go on living?" Jacob and Esau are literally born to conflict; it is a part of their basic equipment. But their parents don't help matters much. Isaac clearly favors his older, more vigorous son, who is a great hunter and who brings him the venison he loves to eat. Rebecca, who has had a vision from God that Jacob will prevail over Esau, favors him. After the story of their birth, the very first thing we learn about the two brothers is that Jacob has tricked Esau out of his birthright. He does this by playing on Esau's impulsive nature. Esau returns famished from a day in the fields, and in keeping with his impulsiveness, he believes he will die if his present hunger persists one moment longer, so he sells his birthright to Jacob for a bowl of red beans.

Esau is ruddy. The beans are red. He has been undone by his own impulsive nature, but he hates Jacob for it nevertheless. Later, when Jacob tricks Esau out of his blessing as well, the rivalry deepens. Isaac is old and his eyesight is getting dim, and he senses that the day of his death is drawing near. He asks Esau to go out and get some venison and cook it for him, so that he can give Esau the innermost blessing of his soul, the final jot of his life force. This blessing is not a mere verbal expression — not just some pro forma well-wishing. It is, rather, an expression of Isaac's gestalt, the complex of spiritual and emotional feeling residing in the deepest recesses of his being. This is why he needs Esau's venison in order to make this blessing. Food is one of our strongest connections to the life core from which Isaac is trying to bless his son.

At a rabbinical retreat once, a man gave me a stress-measuring device called a biodot. The biodot was a tiny piece of paper treated with a chemical that responded to changes in temperature by changing color. The idea was that when we were under stress our fight-or-flight instinct rushed all the blood to the extremities of the body where it would be needed. All this blood rushing to our hands raised the temperature there, so when we were under stress, the biodot registered this change in temperature by turning black. In happier, more relaxed states, the blood settled back into the heart and the inner organs, leaving the hands much cooler. At such times the biodot turned green, and then finally, when we were in the deepest state of relaxation, a radiant, cerulean blue.

Back from the retreat, I watched the biodot changing color as I went about my daily life for several weeks. I noticed, for example, that as soon as I walked into my synagogue, the dot turned a livid, menacing black. It made no difference what I did there. I could pray, I could meditate for hours, but just being in the building threw me into a deep state of stress. Conversely there were activities that were just as dependable for producing that bright blue color that indicated a state of relaxation so deep that it bordered on bliss. Chief among these was eating. Whenever I ate, the biodot turned its most radiant blue. Clearly eating was an activity with profound emotional and spiritual reverberations, and just as clearly it was an activity that resided at the opposite end of the emotional spectrum from stress. Suddenly it seemed pretty obvious why eating so often becomes something other than the simple act of satisfying our hunger. It is nurturance, love, approval: the things Jacob and Esau were really struggling over, the things they had been struggling over in that primal locus of nurturing, the womb.

Isaac needs the food he associates with Esau to carry him to his emotional bedrock, the core of being he wishes to release to Esau with his blessing. But Rebecca overhears Isaac making this request of Esau, and she favors Jacob. So after Esau has gone out to the fields to hunt for venison, she persuades Jacob to deceive his father. He is reluctant to participate in the deception at first, afraid his father will see through it and curse him as a trickster rather than blessing him. As Jacob's life progresses, we will come to see this concern as prophetic, but Rebecca overcomes it by offering to take whatever curses may result from their deception upon herself (a promise she is not empowered to fulfill). Jacob finally agrees to the plan. She will prepare some goat to taste like Esau's venison.

Jacob will dress in Esau's clothing, and cover his smooth hands with the skins of the goats so that he can pass for his hairy brother. Then he will go in and take the blessing his father has intended for Esau.

Isaac is not so easily fooled. He questions Jacob persistently about his identity. "Your voice is the voice of Jacob," he observes, "but your hands are the hands of Esau." But finally the sense of smell is persuasive. Esau's purloined garments are redolent of the fields and not of the flocks and the herds as Jacob's would have been, so Isaac relents and blesses Jacob. It is a blessing of both nurturing and hegemony.

> May God give you of the dew of heaven and the fat of
> the earth.
> Abundance of new grain and wine.
> Let people serve you and nations bow to you:
> Be master over your brothers, and let your mother's sons
> bow to you.
> Cursed be they who curse you, and blessed be they who
> bless you.

When Esau returns from the fields and asks for the blessing his father has promised him, Isaac realizes he has been deceived. Esau cries hysterically and begs his father to bless him too. Isaac blesses him as best he can. He promises him the fat of the earth and the dew of heaven (note that the order was reversed for his brother — heaven was placed before earth, the spiritual before the material) but affirms that Jacob will be master over Esau. Now Esau's resentment of Jacob knows no bounds. He threatens to kill him, and Jacob has to flee for his life.

Jacob will struggle with the consequences of his deception for the rest of his life. He flees to Haran to live with his uncle Lavan, who deceives him continually, a pattern the Torah takes pains to connect to Jacob's own deception of his father. "Your brother came and took your blessing with deception [*b'mirmah*]," Isaac tells Esau when he comes to realize what has happened. "Why have you deceived me [*rimitani*]?" Jacob exclaims when he wakes up to discover that Lavan, who had promised Rachel's hand to him, has placed Leah in his wedding bed instead. *Mirmah* and *rimitani* are both forms of the verb-root *r-m-h*, to trick or deceive. And when Jacob confronts him about this, Lavan makes the connection explicit. "We don't act that way in this place," Lavan explains, "to put the younger before the older."

Lavan will go on tricking Jacob for twenty years, reneging on every deal they make and changing his wages twenty times. After that Jacob will be deceived by his children. His sons will act with guile (again *b'mirmah*) when they circumvent his will and take vengeance on Shechem for the rape of their sister Dinah. And the long Joseph narrative turns on one deception after another: Jacob's sons deceive him about Joseph's fate in the pit; Joseph later deceives his brothers about his identity; and Jacob suffers for all of it. It is as if Jacob's original deception goes out into the world and then constantly comes back to him, as if the world against which he is always struggling is a projection of the guile that resides at the center of his psyche. That's why he must wrestle with that mysterious *ish* — that projection of his own inner darkness — at the banks of the Yabok before he can reconcile with his brother, Esau. The roots of that conflict are within him — his own distorted need for love, approval, and respect — and if he fails to acknowledge them, he will just go on projecting them onto one figure in his life after another.

•

The Torah reinforces this point with an apparent digression about Isaac, which it places between Jacob's two deceptions of his brother, Esau — the stealing of his birthright and the usurping of his blessing. Driven by famine, Isaac, the father of Jacob and Esau, has settled in the land of the Philistines as his father, Abraham, had done a generation before. And also like Abraham, Isaac falls into conflict with the Philistines. Conflict is repetitive and continuous. The same conflicts replicate themselves from generation to generation, in this case, over wells.

What is a well? A well is something that nourishes us, that slakes our thirst. A well is something that goes deep beneath the surface until it reaches the source of life. The spiritual analogy is so obvious, it seems to me, that it hardly requires articulation. All the great biblical romances begin at wells, all the great couples meet there. So wells connect us to the source of life. Wells bring us to love.

And wells are the source of conflict. When we fight, we do not fight about unimportant things. Whatever we may seem to be fighting about on the surface of our lives, when we go deep down, it always turns out that we are fighting about the source of life. We are fighting about love.

"Isaac dug again the wells of water which they had dug in the days of Abraham his father, for the Philistines had stopped them up after the death of Abraham. And he called them names after the names which his father had called them." We learn from this that these names are a big deal. That Isaac insists on using the same names as the previous generation did indicates that they are a source of an older wisdom he wants to remember.

"And Isaac's servants dug in the valley and found there a well of living water. And the herdsmen of Gerar strove with Isaac's herdsmen, saying, This water is ours. And he called the name of the well Esek, because they contended with him."

Esek is a word that indicates objective conflict — contention that takes place outside in the world. It means also to be engaged, as in business or the study of Torah; but the point is, it clearly assumes a subject and an object, and in the case of conflict, something that takes place between two separate parties out in the world.

But the name of the second well they contend for suggests something quite different. "And they dug another well, and they strove for that also, and he called the name of it Sitnah." *Sitnah* means "enmity," but it is a subjective word. It refers to the propensity for conflict that resides in our own breast. It is related to the word Satan, which in the Hebrew tradition means not a demon with a tail and a pitchfork, but rather the inner adversary, the inner accuser — or in Stephen Mitchell's wonderful phrase, the one who expresses God's doubts about his own creation, namely us. So with the naming of the second well, Isaac's understanding of the conflict seems to have shifted. He no longer sees it primarily as a conflict between him and someone else, someone on the outside; rather he is beginning to see it as a conflict with roots in his own heart. Even if he has not caused the conflict, he is at least complicit in it.

We are always complicit in the conflicts we engage in. Even if the conflict is completely provoked by people or events outside us, something in us causes us to engage with the conflict. The world is full of schmohawks. People provoke us all the time, but we only respond to some of these provocations and not to others, because there is something in our own inner life that is touched by them, that rises to the bait. We usually learn that this is so just as Isaac did — through the repetition of circumstances: "And they dug another well, and they strove for that also." When we go from situation to situation, and we realize that the same kind of conflicts have followed us from place to place, we begin to get a glimmering that the problem might be within us and not just in the circumstances. There is no sudden insight, no revelation that leads Isaac to realize that the source of his conflict is within and not without — it is simply that the circumstances have changed but the conflict remains. This is what teaches him that the conflict has not derived from the circumstances, but rather from his own heart.

It is the same with Jacob. It is the simple accumulation — the reiteration — of conflict and not some sudden flash of insight or understanding that leads him to finally confront his own darkness at the bank of the Yabok. The characters and the objects of conflict keep changing: first there is Esau, then his father, then Lavan; first the birthright is in contention, then the blessing, then the issue of whether he will marry Rachel or Leah, then the question of how many sheep he will have, then his wages. The people and places and circumstances keep changing. The only thing that remains constant is the contention itself, replicating itself in every situation, projecting itself onto all the people in his life. After a while, after ten or twenty or thirty years, one begins to notice this.

I have lived in many places in the course of my life. I have had many jobs, been in many relationships, studied in many schools. But wherever I have gone, I have found myself in an adversarial relationship with someone, a rivalry for attention and approval. This happened when I was living among the poets of San Francisco in the late 1960s; in the midst of the Zen world I inhabited in the 1970s, despite all its nonadversarial rhetoric; at rabbinical school and at every congregation I ever served as a rabbi — it happened with cantors, with synagogue presidents, with other rabbis. In every case I found myself set against someone, felt insulted or slighted by them, felt they weren't according me enough attention or respect, felt that others had been fooled by them, that if they really saw through these people as I did, they would never give them so much attention and admiration. Instead they would give these things to me. Many of the people I found myself fighting with this way really were quite awful. They were disrespectful, dishonest, ambitious, competitive, mean-spirited, and self-obsessed. I had good taste in enemies. But why was I always engaged with these people? Why did they always get my goat? Why me and not someone else? It didn't take too many changes in scenery before this question began to assert itself to me. As my meditation practice deepened, the question became more and more compelling. Often, when I sat down on the cushion, I became aware that there was a constant debate going on in my psyche between me and these adversaries. Just below the level of conscious thought, I was constantly building my case against them, proving that they had hurt me maliciously, that they hadn't given me my due.

Eventually these arguments gave way and images from my childhood began to emerge, images of abandonment and neglect. Now anyone who knew my parents at all would no doubt be shocked to hear this. My father and mother were extremely loving parents. In fact my mother had an almost preternatural capacity for nurturing and giving love. Distant relatives, acquaintances from her distant past who were in trouble of one sort or another, were always calling and coming to see her for support. People saw her as that kind of figure, and she really was. I had a close friend who was hospitalized with a serious illness, and one night when things looked quite dark, when he began to lose faith that he would ever recover, he summoned his last ounce of strength and said to his wife, "Get Charlotte Lew on the phone." This was supremely odd. He barely knew my mother. They had only a distant acquaintance. But something deep in him had identified her as a person who could nourish him, to whom he could turn in this moment of desperate need. And the fact is, he called her, she talked to him, and it helped him pull through this desperate time.

So my mother was certainly not deficient as a nurturer, and she genuinely loved me, of this I am sure. But my mother had a lot on her plate, and not just the usual rush of activity that accompanied the frantic ascent from Depression-era poverty to upper-middle-class social prominence that she, as so many in her generation, was in the process of making. All during my childhood, both my father and my younger sister were terribly ill. There were many times when both of them were in the hospital at the same time, and my mother would spend her days rushing back and forth between them. Consequently I was often left to fend for myself, alone in an empty house, or by the side of a lonely road. Oddly, many of the images of abandonment that would flood my mind during these meditations had to do with carpooling. We lived four miles outside the nearest town, and like most suburban kids I required constant chauffeuring to and from school, piano lessons, baseball games, parties, and play dates with friends. During these years of crisis, when my mother was overwhelmed with the demands on her time, she was constantly late, and I would often spend hours waiting to be picked up, praying in vain that the next car would be hers. Or she would drop me off hours early, and I would wait alone for the game to start or the lesson to begin. Even then I understood, at least on the conscious level. But deep down I felt abandoned and humiliated. Now my mother is in the advanced stages of Alzheimer's disease, and this early sense of abandonment often comes flooding back to me as I sit gazing into her stony, unresponsive eyes, or when I tell her I love her on the telephone and she says nothing in return.

I understand very well that all of this was the result of the difficult circumstances my mother had to deal with and not a deficiency in her love for me, but I think that even without these special difficulties, it is still likely that I would have felt a certain disappointment with the quality of her affection. There is something inherently disappointing about parental love. Even the most loving parents never seem to love us enough, to live up to our expectation of how much they should love us. I think that as children, some part of us expects that our parents should love us infinitely and constantly, to the exclusion of any concerns of their own. This never happens, of course, and we are disappointed, and this is not such a bad thing. It is this very disappointment that propels us out into the world to find someone who will love us this way, or as the book of Genesis has it, "Therefore, a man shall leave his father and mother and shall cleave to his wife, and they will become one flesh." A spouse or a lover is more likely (although hardly guaranteed) to be able to provide us with this kind of love. But even they will disappoint us in the end. Love on this earth, after all, is inevitably finite. I love my wife in the most tender way imaginable, and I feel her love for me absolutely, but there is something heartbreaking about this feeling. We have been married for more than twenty years, and I still feel like melting whenever I see her. The words "I love you" leak out of me all day long but never manage to express what I really mean, what I really feel, which is something infinite and inexpressible. At the same time, I am haunted by a tragic sense that all this will be snatched away from me someday, at least in this world. Love constantly brings us to the brink of the infinite, yet no sooner does love arise than it brings in its wake the painful realization that it will end, that we will die.

So it is that I find myself fighting with people all the time over scraps of love and attention, that I become vulnerable to their provocations, that they can always touch me in this inner place of lack and draw me into conflict with them. It has very little to do with them. It mostly has to do with me, with the torn and hurting places my heart is trying to cover over, the deep wells my disappointment is trying to stop up.

I have a friend who teaches attorneys to do mediation work. They come from all over the country to study with him, and he employs role-playing and case studies and all kinds of other techniques to teach them his craft. He tells me that whenever they examine a conflict, they always have to go through a three-stage process to get to the bottom of it. First they listen to what everyone is saying — the high moral language in which their claims against each other are invariably couched. Then they come to understand that the conflicts do not, in fact, revolve around these moral issues at all, but rather around the resentment, anger, and antipathy the combatants have come to feel toward each other. But that is not the end of the process either. Inevitably there is something beneath that too, something beneath the anger and the resentment and the jealousy, and that is the simple fact that all parties to the conflict are suffering. All are watching the world they inhabit slip away from them. All need love desperately and either can't find it or have found it but realize deep down that it won't last forever. Reality is hard to take at its core. So they strike out. They strike out at each other, because they can't bear to acknowledge the truth of their lives. Real mediation begins, my friend told me, when the focus of the mediator shifts from the claims of the parties in the conflict to their suffering. That's when they begin to make headway as mediators. That's when the conflicts begin to resolve.

Our suffering is not really *our* suffering. It does not belong to us. It is part of the great wellspring of suffering common to all human beings. And it doesn't always have a cause either, not even one rooted in the past which we inappropriately project onto the present. Quite often our subjective impulses are disconnected from any cause at all, either past or present.

A woman from my meditation center came to speak to me recently. Her son suffered from acute mental illness and had been chronically homeless for several years. But she didn't come to me to talk about that. There was very little left to say about her son's situation except that her heart had been utterly broken by it. As far as anyone could see, there was nothing she could do about it either. God knows she had tried all available remedies — therapy, social services, legal compulsion — to no avail. This day she wanted to talk to me about a technical practice issue, her visual experience in meditation. In most of the meditation centers she had attended before, people sat facing the wall, but at Makor Or we sit facing one another, and this was causing a problem for her. In our meditation we sit with eyes neither opened nor closed, but rather kind of half opened, looking at the visual field without really focusing on it. We don't want to close our eyes, because then we become prone to drifting off into an unfocused reverie. On the other hand we don't want to attach our mind to the objects of sight either. We want to focus on the breath and the body. When facing the wall as she did at home and at other meditation centers, she found that it worked for her to focus on a single point on the wall, a technique commonly taught by meditation instructors. But at Makor Or she was finding this impossible to do. The people in her line of vision were far too distracting. She couldn't reduce them to a single point as she could with a spot on the wall, especially if they were fidgeting or otherwise moving about as they so frequently were. This troubled her, because when she could avoid such distractions her inner visual landscape invariably came into focus, and she found this to be a fascinating place where the play of light and shape was infinitely various. She found it both easier and more pleasurable to meditate with the visual images that arose spontaneously within her than with those that seemed to have been provoked by the external world.

Then she told me something else. Lately, in spite of all the tragedy regarding her son, she had been experiencing periods of deep joy in meditation. This joy just seemed to well up in her heart without any cause that she was aware of, but it was quite profound and it often endured for some time. She didn't connect this observation to the one she had made about her visual field, but I did. What both the visual and emotional effects she was speaking of had in common, it seemed to me, was that they seemed to have arisen in her subjective field out of nothing, with no external cause or stimulus. With our relentlessly psychological orientation, we might be inclined to attribute this woman's joy to denial, sublimation, or compensation. But these are not the only possibilities. It might just as easily have arisen for no reason at all other than the fact that feelings of all kinds are constantly rising up and falling away within us.

Sometimes we get into conflicts because we project feelings onto the present that have their roots in some trauma from the past. But sometimes the feelings we project onto the present have no cause at all. They just arise in our hearts, and believing that they must belong somewhere, we attach them to a conflict with others. Anger just wells up, but because we assume it must have a cause, we project it onto someone else and begin to fight with him. Sometimes ocean waves are caused by the wind, and sometimes by the gravitational pull of the moon. But even when there is no wind or when the pull of the moon is too weak to be felt, waves continue to rise and fall for no other reason than that there is an ocean whose nature it is to swell and to subside. Similarly, it is the nature of mind to produce a tide of thought and feeling.

Our suffering is not really our suffering. It does not belong to us, nor does it always have a cause in the objective world. Often it is simply a part of a boundless sea on which impulses and feelings ebb and flow without cause. And the moment when we become aware of this is the moment that the sense of being constricted by conflict begins to give way to a feeling of spaciousness and the end of conflict altogether.

There is an echo of the earlier dispute between Abraham's herdsmen and those of Lot in the story of Isaac and the wells. In both cases the quarrel arises because there are too many flocks and not enough land or water to support them. Just before the dispute over the wells breaks out, Isaac is told to leave by the Philistine king because his large retinue is causing anxiety among the Philistines.

So the sense of being hemmed in, constricted by a narrow space, is characteristic of this conflict from the beginning. It is characteristic, I think, of all conflict. Conflict hems us in. Conflict constricts us. It oppresses us and constricts our vision to a single point of hostile focus. We see ourselves as the inhabitants of a narrow space with not enough sustenance to support us. We feel that life is a zero-sum game in which we have to fight others for sustenance, for space, and for love.

As Isaac relocates the source of this conflict in his own breast, both the conflict and this sense of zero-sum constriction disappear. "And he moved from there, and dug another well, and they did not strive with him over this one, so he called the name of it Rechovot [spaciousness], and he said, For now the Lord has made room for us and we will be fruitful in the land." Now God has made room. God has made room in the land for both Isaac and the Philistines, and God has made room in Isaac's heart for the feelings that seemed so oppressive to him a short while ago. There is room for them precisely because they are not being hemmed in from without. They are not being hemmed in by anything.

In meditation we let go of each breath, and as we do we feel the boundaries of our being giving way as well. Our personal space becomes larger with each exhale, until finally the heart becomes boundless. Unfettered by the limitations that it imagines to be coming at it from the outside, the heart is free to express the deep wellsprings of feeling that the sense of being in conflict has stopped up. We are truly fish athirst in the water. Unfettered by conflict, the heart is free to plunge into the infinite pool of suffering that we inhabit with all being and, beyond that, into the bottomless wellspring of love that informs every moment of our experience and saturates everything in creation — the love that brings the next breath into our body of its own accord whenever we breath out, the love that faithfully leads us down the freeway off-ramp to a street and not into some dark void, the love that holds us down to this earth, and circulates our blood, and spins the stars in their spirals.

In these first stories the Bible tells about the origin of conflict, contention moves from the inside out. It begins in the heart, then projects itself onto our relationships with others, and then spreads heart to heart until it has filled the world. It begins with the simple desire for the one thing we cannot have, which pulls us out of paradise and into a world of conflict, suffering, and death.

But when we are speaking about the healing of conflict, we move from the outside in. We begin already enmeshed in conflict with others, and we try to locate the inner source of this conflict, the heart-thread that snagged us, that got us caught up in it. When we finally do, everything gives way. We realize there is no "other" hemming us in, and our heart suddenly finds itself in a wide-open space. There is a well in this place. Its opening is very broad and it reaches very far down.

PRACTICE POINTS

Disarming the Inner Roots of Conflict

The inner roots of conflict express themselves in our minds in various subjective forms. Two forms I have found particularly fruitful to work with are argument and antipathy. Arguments are constantly going on in our minds; antipathy toward various people and circumstances is constantly arising there as well. When we come to realize that these arguments and these feelings are not what they seem to be, we have taken a big step toward disarming the inner tendency toward external conflict.

When we first begin meditating and begin to become conscious of the functioning of our mind, we may be amazed at how much of our mental activity seems to be given over to arguments. After a while we begin to notice that the structure of the arguments is far more significant than their content. The arguments seem to take two basic forms. We defend ourselves against unjust attacks by others, or we argue that we deserve more credit and attention than we are getting from various people in our lives. As our focus continues we begin to notice that while the people we are arguing with and the content of the arguments change all the time, the forms remain constant. It is as if these argumentative structures have been hardwired into our brain and just keep repeating themselves like some kind of manic tape loop. In our usual unmindful state, we are prone to taking the content of the arguments at face value. Out in our lives, we are truly angry at the people we feel have accused us unjustly or failed to give us proper credit.

Only after watching the forms of these arguments rise up over and over again, each time with a different cast of characters and particulars, does it begin to occur to us that neither the characters nor the particulars are the point; the argument itself is the point. The template is there in our mind already, and all we have to do is fill it in with a few names and facts.

Simply watching this process unfold, the same old argumentative forms rising up in our mind and then filling themselves in with names and details as becomes necessary, begins to disarm the process. Realizing that these arguments have no inherent content but are just forms, habitual mental structures, makes us a lot less likely to take them seriously, to pursue the conflicts they lead us into with other people. Consciousness changes everything. Just being aware of this inner structural root of conflict will often prevent the conflict itself from arising.

The same is true of antipathy. When we first feel strong dislike or hatred rising up in our mind, we really believe it is inherently connected to its object, a particular person or circumstance we dislike or detest. But after we witness the same feeling arising in our mind with many different objects, we realize that it is the feeling itself and not the object that is essential. The antipathy is in us. And as we watch this feeling rise up over and over again in meditation, we begin to lose faith in this antipathy. We stop believing in it, and it begins to lose its hold over us.

So watching the internal markers of conflict can be an extremely fruitful focus of our practice. Watching the inner argument, watching antipathy, watching anger, watching feelings of jealousy and hurt as they arise in the mind, it becomes increasingly clear that they are essentially internal experiences, structures our own psyche has generated, and that the conflicts we experience in the external world are products of these structures, exercises in shadowboxing. The more we become aware of these structures, the more they begin to lose their power over us. Eventually they will fall away altogether, and the conflicts they engendered in our life will cease to arise.

Patterns of Conflict

Another marker of the inner roots of conflict is the repetitive patterns that occur in the various spheres of our life. We may have a particular kind of conflict in a relationship, leave the relationship because of it, and then find we have the identical problem in our next relationship and in the one after that. We may fall into a dispute at work. The person we were at odds with leaves the office, but before very long we find we are enmeshed in a similar conflict with another of our coworkers. These patterns are a fairly reliable sign that the cause of the conflict is within. As they disclose themselves in meditation, we can use them as pointers to the kinds of subjective forms we spoke of in the last practice point — the arguments, antipathy, anger, jealousy, and hurt that arise consistently in our mind. As we notice conflict repeating itself in our life, we can accustom ourself to shifting our focus from the external conflicts to their inner roots, and in this way we can begin to break these patterns.

Chapter Four

Don't Be Afraid!

1. A Five-Step Program: Don't Panic, Pull Yourself Together, See Clearly, Be Still, and Get Going

ANOTHER FORM OF SUFFERING, ANOTHER DEEP WELL OF feeling that our conflicts cover over, is fear. The English word "fear" (like the words "pain" and "suffering") is quite imprecise and really denotes a complex variety of feelings. There are two Hebrew words for fear — *pachad* and *norah* — and although these words are often used interchangeably, they roughly correspond to two very different spiritual states.

Pachad refers to projected or imagined fear. According to

Rebbe Nachman, suffering is the state of being afraid of something that we don't have to be afraid of. This is *pachad,* the fear of the phantom, the fear whose object is imagined. It is astounding how often such fears become the organizing principles of our lives and how much they close us off from the world.

Norah is a very different kind of fear. It is the fear that overcomes us when we suddenly find ourselves in possession of considerably more energy than we are used to, inhabiting a larger space than we are used to inhabiting. What are God's most common opening words when addressing mortals? *Al tirei* — Don't be afraid. *Tirei* is a form of the word *norah.* The commentators often speculate as to why God says this. In each case they try to figure out what the people God is addressing might be afraid of, since it is rarely self-evident. But the obvious answer that covers all these cases, it seems to me, is that the people are afraid of God. The nearness of God is an experience of an intensity, an energy, and a sense of spaciousness that they are not accustomed to, and it occasions a sense of *norah,* a mixture of fear and awe. A new strength announces itself, a new energy bristles through our body, and we call this bristling energy fear, or *norah,* for lack of a better term. *Norah* is trying to push us open. The fear we experience at such times is simply our resistance to this opening.

The leave-taking process we have mentioned a number of times already engages both kinds of fear. Fear, in fact, is both an important cause and an important result of this process. Often *pachad,* the fear of an imagined object, is what we need to take leave of, and the process of leave-taking itself brings us into engagement with *norah* — an opening, a sudden vulnerability to a new strength.

The ultimate leave-taking story in the Torah — Israel's seminal leave-taking, in fact — is the exodus from Egypt. Like the individual leave-taking stories we spoke of earlier, this one begins with a flight from suffering and ends with an encounter with the transcendent. The Children of Israel flee Egypt, the place of constriction, the house of bondage, the locus of all their fears, and three months later, as a direct consequence of this departure, God speaks to them directly, revealing the Torah to them at Mount Sinai. But as we mentioned earlier, this leave-taking departs from the archetypal model in at least one critical respect. In the other such stories (Jacob's ladder, Jacob and the angel, Moses and the burning bush; Jesus, Muhammad, Buddha, and so forth), an individual takes leave of the community and encounters the transcendent in midflight. Here everyone leaves, and everyone encounters the transcendent. As a result, from this moment on Judaism is inescapably communal. *Al tifrotz min ha tzibur* — do not separate yourself from the community — becomes the reigning taboo, and the idea of leave-taking undergoes a reinterpretation. It must now become internalized. Leave-taking no longer means packing a suitcase and leaving town. Rather, it refers to an inner process, leaving the scattered and confused consciousness we usually occupy and entering a more focused and mindful state.

The precise moment that the Children of Israel take leave of Egypt — when they take an epochal leap of faith and cast off into the Red Sea itself — is described in some detail in the book of Exodus, and this description provides a wonderful paradigm for how to face fear, how to face those critical moments in life when we know we have to do something but we have no idea what to do. It breaks the act of leave-taking into five distinct parts, and in so doing, offers a five-step program — five clear verbs uttered in rapid succession, the first four by Moses and the last one by God — that provides a map we can follow to help us negotiate such moments as they occur in our own lives.

Such moments are often awash in terror, and this is certainly the case in this account of the moment when the Children of Israel stand at the lip of the sea. They have only recently experienced the horror of the ten plagues, which climaxed with the Night of Watching, a terrifying time in which the Angel of Death passed through every doorway in Egypt and the horrific screams of the dying Egyptian first-born filled the air. The next morning, at the urging of his people, Pharaoh finally relents and lets the Israelites go. But no sooner are they gone than Pharaoh thinks better of things. "What is this we have done," he asks his court, "releasing Israel from our service?" So Pharaoh orders his army after Israel, and they overtake Israel camped by the edge of the sea. When the Israelites see the Egyptians coming after them on the horizon, they fly into a panic and they say to Moses, "Weren't there enough graves in Egypt that you had to take us out here to the desert to die?" (This line was, no doubt, uttered by the karmic ancestor of Henny Youngman.) "Isn't this exactly what we were talking about in Egypt when we said 'Let us be and we'll serve the Egyptians, because it is better to serve the Egyptians than to die in the desert'?"

This is the critical moment, and extremely familiar to each of us. We are stuck. We are being pressed. Pharaoh's army is coming after us and there's nowhere to go but into the sea. One of our children is failing in school or in life or in both and we have no idea how to help them. The bills must be paid but we don't have enough money in the bank to pay them. We love our spouse desperately but our marriage continues to deteriorate no matter what we do, or how hard we try to make things better. Our job is driving us into a deep depression and we just don't feel that we can go on, but we don't know how we would make ends meet — how we would support our family — without it. We have to do something and we have no idea what to do, so we panic.

Here Moses and God conspire to give us a program for negotiating such moments — the five-step program I mentioned above.

> But Moses said to the people, "**Don't be afraid** [*Al tira-u*]. **Collect yourselves** [*Hityatzvu*] and **see** [*uru*] the salvation which Adonai will make for you today. . . . Adonai will fight for you and you will **be still** [*tacharishun*]." Then Adonai said to Moses, "Why do you cry out to me? Tell the Israelites to **just get going** [*v'yisa-u*]." [Emphasis added.]

First of all, Moses says, don't be afraid, meaning not so much, don't feel afraid — that can't be helped — but rather, don't act on your fear, don't panic, don't go running around after your fear, because chances are you are running around after a phantom.

There is a famous anomaly in the passage that describes the Egyptian pursuit of Israel. In one sentence it says that the Egyptians pursued the Children of Israel, both verb and subject in the plural. But only two sentences later, it says that Egypt ran after Israel (both subject and verb in the singular). Why does the Torah shift number so cavalierly here? According to Rashi, it is because the Torah wishes to emphasize what it was the Israelites saw when they raised their eyes to the horizon. They saw not the Egyptians themselves, in the plural, but the spirit of Egypt, in the singular. They saw their idea of Egypt. They saw the Egypt in which they had cowered as slaves for four hundred years, in which they were abused and outnumbered. In other words, they saw their fear of Egypt. They saw a mental construct, or in Rebbe Nachman's words, something that they were afraid of but didn't have to be.

The biblical text takes pains to make the same point. This text is ambiguous about exactly how many chariots there were in the army that had pinned the Israelites down at the sea. The Torah tells us that Pharaoh sent "600 choice chariots, and all the chariots in Egypt" after the Israelites, and that each of the chariots had three Egyptian soldiers in it. Were there 600 chariots in all, or 600 choice chariots and a larger number of ordinary chariots? In the first case, that would mean there would be a total of 1,800 Egyptians chasing after Israel, in the second, there would be an indeterminate number. But even multiplying this number by ten, there would be 18,000 Egyptians, and by 100 (a highly unlikely multiplier), 180,000.

But even in the worst and most unlikely case, there were several million Israelites at the shore of the sea: 600,000 men of fighting age, as we learn in the several censuses that are undertaken in the Torah, and at least two and a half times that many in total population. Why would such a tremendous throng be afraid of 1,800, or even 180,000, charioteers? The answer is that they were not responding to what was really there, nor even to what they saw. Rather they were responding to a phantom. They were responding to a fear-inducing product of their own imagination.

It is often the case that we are held in thrall by such phantoms, by false beliefs about our lives, by paralyzing myths. One of the most significant leave-takings in my own life was the night I decided to leave law school. My parents had always believed that there were only two possibilities for me in life, to become a doctor or a lawyer. Becoming a doctor was by far the preferred course, but failing that, becoming a lawyer was an acceptable, albeit disappointing alternative. But that was as far as they were prepared to take their disappointment. Anything "less" than that was utterly unacceptable, and this was made clear to me from birth. All through my school years, I had a calamitous relationship with the entire field of science, and medicine very quickly ceased to be a viable option. So I wound up in law school, but that was not a very good fit either. I barely made it through my first year, excelling at criminal and constitutional law, but barely passing contracts, torts, procedure, et al. The second year, we embarked upon the study of the Uniform Commercial Code, and by November I knew I was finished. I was overwhelmed. If I didn't drop out voluntarily, I would surely flunk out after the first round of December exams. I screwed up all my courage and called my parents to tell them about my decision. My father reviled me, my mother wept as if I had told her that I had come down with some dreaded disease, and they both let me know in no uncertain terms that I had let them down very badly. I hung up the phone and lay on the sofa for the rest of the night and waited to die. I was sure I would die. It was impossible to imagine a life beyond my parents' expectations, so I lay awake and waited for my death with more resignation than fear. I was quite surprised when the morning came and I was still alive. I count my real life as having begun then. Before that morning, I had been hemmed in by my fear of a phantom, not permitting myself to imagine a life that it was actually possible for me to live.

So this is *al tira-u,* the first step on this five-step program: Don't be afraid. Don't panic. Don't spend your life fleeing phantoms, don't go scattering to the farthest corners of your consciousness to escape things you only imagine you need to escape.

The second step is *hityatzvu* — pull yourself together, take a stand, collect yourself, constitute yourself, bring your awareness in from all the corners of mind where it is usually scattered. This word is derived etymologically from a Ugaritic word for construction, building, in the sense of gathering materials together, concentrating them in a single place, and then standing them up.

When we sit down to meditate, the first thing we notice is that our awareness is scattered in a thousand places; our mind is unfocused, flung all over the place, full of anxiety, anger, and every other conceivable emotional impulse. *Hityatzvu* corresponds to the inhale, when we follow the momentum of the in-breath and bring our awareness in from all the places it has been scattered. The first step — *al tira-u* — corresponds to the exhale. We breathe out and we let go of everything we are holding on to that is no longer real. Breathing in again, we reconstitute ourselves. We allow our world to re-create itself anew. We bring our awareness in and we take a stand at the center of our breathing in the sense that we stand firm with our experience; we don't try to avoid it, even the aspects of it that might frighten us. Rather we inhabit our lives, we fill them with our awareness. We stop running and squirming in the face of our phantoms and we stand still.

The consequence of this resolute standing firm — standing with — is that we begin to see our experience as it really is rather than as we have imagined it to be. The dream — the nightmare — that has held us in its thrall begins to dissipate as we stare it down, and the real lineaments of our experience begin to emerge. This is the third of the five steps — *uru,* seeing. When we stop running around after our imagination, we begin to see our experience as it really is. Breathing out, we let go of the world we have imagined. Breathing in, the life we actually inhabit begins to emerge, to take shape. Lying still on that sofa that night, being still with the imaginary fear that I was going to die if I quit law school and thereby stopped living the life my parents needed me to live, I saw my life clearly for the first time. I saw that I was not bound by the limitations I had imagined, that I was much freer, and that my life was full of many more possibilities than I had thought.

There is a story in the second book of Kings (7:3–20) that celebrates the special vision of the outsider, the wonderful capacity for seeing reality that comes to us when we have taken leave. The Aramaeans have had the Israelite city of Samran under siege for some time. Four lepers, involuntary leave-takers, have been excluded from the city, as lepers always are. Panic and hunger have begun to afflict the inhabitants of Samran, but outside the city the lepers' prospects are even worse. None of the Israelites will venture outside to feed them, and they are beginning to starve. Finally, in desperation, the lepers decide to throw themselves upon the mercy of their enemies, the Aramaeans. They will enter the Aramaean camp and beg for food. If, as is likely, the Aramaeans slaughter them, so what? They will soon die of starvation anyway. But when they enter the Aramaean camp, they find it to be empty. The Aramaeans are no longer there. The city of Samran is now being held in siege by a product of its own imagination, a phantom, but only the outsiders, the ones who had taken leave, were capable of seeing this.

The fourth step is *tacharishun* — be still. Stillness is both the cause and the product of this kind of vision. When we stand still and stop running away from our phantoms, we acquire the capacity to see the world as it is, and the act of seeing the world as it is — seeing the world with our own eyes — brings a deep stillness in its wake. First there is the *standing* still, an action that we take, and then there is *being* still, a condition, a state of being that comes over us as a consequence of our action. This second stillness — the state of being rather than the action — comes about both because we are no longer reacting to imaginary fears and because there is something about being present, about seeing the world as it is, that produces a stillness on its own. This stillness becomes the field of our salvation. We know we must do something, and we have no idea what to do, but when we reach this point of deep stillness, the next act seems to rise up of its own accord. This is why it is significant that while Moses utters the first four verbs of our five-step program, God utters the fifth: *v'yisa-u*. Just get going. Just act. Just do it.

There seems to be some tension between Moses's last utterance — be still — and God's imperative to get going. At first blush, in fact, God seems to be contradicting Moses. Moses has said, "**[1] Don't be afraid. [2] Collect yourselves** and **[3] see** the salvation which Adonai will make for you today. . . . Adonai will fight for you and you will **[4] be still.**" But then God says, "Why do you cry out to me? Tell the Israelites to **[5] just get going.**" Considering this verse more carefully, however, we see that God is responding not to Moses, but to the Youngmanesque cry of despair the Israelites uttered ("Weren't there enough graves in Egypt?"). Moses himself was responding to this cry, and God is simply affirming or completing his response. There is no real contradiction between Moses's suggestion to be still and God's command to get going. The stillness is, in fact, the ground out of which this going must arise. What the Torah seems to be hinting at here is something akin to the Taoist idea of Wu Wei, or nonaction.

In the 1960's, when my friends and I first encountered the idea of Wu Wei, we thought it was the greatest thing since sliced bread, because it seemed to offer the perfect justification for the way we were already living. We were already practicing Wu Wei. We were doing absolutely nothing. We were just sitting around goofing and listening to music all day long, and here was a Taoist doctrine that seemed to support this life of nonaction. It was one of the great disappointments of my life when I discovered that this wasn't really what Wu Wei meant at all. Really, Wu Wei meant doing things without the sense that you were the doer — egoless doing. It meant that the action arose of its own accord, and not out of some decision you made. And Wu Wei always arose out of stillness, as it was only in stillness that the next inevitable action you needed to take could declare itself, that the chatter of the world and your own mind could quiet down enough so that you could hear the voice of God.

Wu Wei is doing what must be done next. It is action in perfect alignment with the moment. God will fight for you, but you — that is to say your ego — will be quiet. Wu Wei is the absolutely necessary action. When the mind is clear, we feel both this action and its necessity unmistakably. We know we must leave one job and take another. We know the time has come to leave our marriage. After many months of uncertainty and indecision, we suddenly feel it for a certainty in the marrow of our bones. After weeks of trying to reason our way out of a dilemma, or to coax its solution out of hiding by the force of our own will, we stop trying to force the issue, and the sea parts of its own volition.

We find ourselves in a terrible dilemma and we are appropriately frightened. We know something must be done, but we have no idea what, and this terrifies us. So (1) *al tira-u* — we stop running away from our fear; (2) *hityatzvu* — we collect ourselves, we stand still, we let go of our terror, and we allow the world to reconstitute itself. Then (3) *uru* — we see our experience for what it really is; and (4) *tacharishun* — this brings us to a point of deep stillness. Only then does the next action — the necessary action — arise out of this stillness, and (5) *v'yisa-u* — we move forward, not really acting ourselves, but giving ourselves to the action the moment requires.

This is how we discover what we must do next when we have no idea of this ourselves. This is what we do when we find ourselves flung and scattered to the distant corners of our consciousness, fleeing *pachad*, a fear of something that isn't real.

2. Become Who You Are!

So much for *pachad*, that fear of the imaginary, of the thing we don't need to be afraid of, which Rebbe Nachman sees as the root of all suffering. But what about *norah*, the sudden and frightening eruption of a new strength, the feeling that we are possessed of far more energy than we can handle, that our reality is not as bounded as we thought, but frighteningly boundless? What about that terrifying sense that our life is far more intense than we imagined, that we are far more powerful, and far more vulnerable to loss, than we supposed? What about that fear that fills the pit of our stomach when we suddenly find ourself in the midst of the most important transformation of all — the process of becoming who we are?

The idea that we are in the process of becoming who we are is often spoken of in terms of fulfilling our destiny. I am often asked if Judaism subscribes to the idea of destiny, and if so, how does it square with the doctrine of free will, which has such prominence of place in Jewish theology?

The answer to the first question is yes. And when it comes to the apparent contradiction between destiny and free will, the answer is that we Jews have our cake and eat it too. Everything is foreseen, and free will is always in your hands, declared Rabbi Akivah in *Pirke Avot*. But how could this be? If everything is foreseen, if we all have an immutable destiny, what could it possibly mean to say that we also have free will?

A story from the Talmud about this same Rabbi Akivah begins to point us toward an answer. On the day that Rabbi Akivah's daughter was born, astrologers told him that she would be killed by a poisonous snake on the morning of her wedding day. Many years pass. On the morning in question, Rabbi Akivah is watching his daughter get dressed for her wedding. She pulls a large hairpin out of the dressing room wall and lo and behold, a poisonous snake is impaled on the end of the pin.

What did you do? Rabbi Akivah asks. Well, last night, while everyone else was enjoying themselves at the prenuptial feast, his daughter replies, a beggar came knocking at the kitchen door, but the celebration was so raucous that nobody heard him. I heard him, though, and I opened the door and fed him.

His daughter's answer illuminates Rabbi Akivah's question. When he said, "What did you do?" he meant, "What good deed did you perform to avert the death that was decreed for you this morning?" The assumption of this question is far-reaching. It implies that while we clearly have a destiny — his daughter was certainly destined to die, as the presence of the poisonous snake in her dressing room attests — that destiny is not fixed. It is fluid and subject to our behavior. When Rabbi Akivah's daughter fed the beggar at the door, she altered the course of her destiny.

So according to the tradition, we really do have a destiny, but the question of whether or not we live out that destiny is in our own hands. We can alter a negative destiny by the force of our righteous intention. On the other hand, we can choose not to become the person we were destined to be. Everything is foreseen, and free will is always in our hands.

Ebo tribesmen have a custom of standing over their sleeping children at night and whispering in their ears, "Become who you are! Become who you are!" because they intuit that it isn't inevitable. If they didn't know deep down that the issue was in doubt, they wouldn't have to say it.

But the issue is in doubt for all of us. We do have a destiny, but we might choose not to live it out. In fact most of us may very well make this choice, because save for the fear of death itself, there is no greater fear than that of being who we are, of living out the life it has been given us to live.

The question of destiny manifests itself most clearly in two areas of our lives, love and work. The idea that the person we love is destined for us is one of the oldest claims of our tradition. But the idea that each of us has an indispensable contribution to make to the larger flow of life is an even older claim.

Let's look at love first. We meet Abraham and Sarah when they are already married, so the very first Jewish love story is the romance between their son Isaac and his wife, Rebecca. This story positively reeks of destiny. Abraham sends his servant back to Haran to find a wife for his son Isaac. This servant is terrified that he won't make the right choice, so he prays to God for a sign. If I go to Haran and I come to the well there, and I see a beautiful young woman and she offers me water, and then she offers to take care of my camels too, then I'll know I have the right woman. All this comes to pass. Rebecca, a beautiful woman, meets him at the well, offers him water, and takes care of his camels. She is obviously Isaac's intended — his *beshert* — so the servant brings her back to Canaan, and when their caravan is drawing near to Isaac's camp, we read the following:

> And Isaac went out to meditate in the fields just before evening, and he raised his eyes and he saw that camels were coming. At the same moment, Rebecca raised her eyes and she saw Isaac, and she fell from her camel and she said to her servant, "Who is that man who is walking toward us?" . . . And Isaac brought Rebecca into his mother's tent, and he took Rebecca and she became his wife and he loved her.

Talk about love at first sight! The magnetism between Isaac and Rebecca is palpable in this passage and seems to suggest an attraction that is bigger than both of them, as they used to say in the Hollywood movies. The Ba'al Shem Tov, the founder and greatest figure of Hasidic Judaism, used to say that every person has a light going up from the core of their soul all the way to heaven, and when two people who are destined to be together finally meet, their lights join and form a single light that illumines the world.

But this was merely a poetic reformulation of one of the Talmud's fondest sentiments. Stories about lovers being destined for one another abound in the Talmud. In one such, Rabbi Yosi Ben Halafta was giving a Roman noblewoman instruction in the Torah. After she read the very beginning of the Torah, the account of creation in Genesis, she came back to him with a question. "It says in the book of Genesis that God made everything in heaven and earth in seven days," she began. "What I want to know is this: what has God been doing ever since?" "God has been making love matches between people ever since," Yosi Ben Halafta replied, "and it's much more difficult and time-consuming than creating the universe ever was."

In another story, Raba encountered a young man sitting along the roadside weeping. "What's the matter?" he asked. "I am desperately in love with a certain young woman," the young man said, "and I don't know if it's going to work out." "Don't worry," Raba said, "if she's right for you, you can't get away from her. If she's meant for you, it's inevitable." Elsewhere in the Talmud it says that forty days before an embryo is formed, a Bat Kol — a heavenly voice — goes out and proclaims the name of the person that embryo will marry. In another version of this same story, it says that such a Bat Kol goes out from heaven every day of our lives until we've found our intended.

I do dozens of weddings every year, but I only use two frames for wedding speeches, because I have found over the years that while human beings occur in a dazzling variety of forms and personalities, there are basically only two types of couples: those who believe they have been destined for each other and those who do not. There are those who instantly know upon meeting that this is the person they were meant for, and there are those who think their meeting may have been more or less random, but who felt a certain sanctity in the gradual process of coming to love each other, coming to see the sacred in each other and in their relationship. So I have one speech for the first type and another for the second.

Who is right? How do I know? Secretly I think they are both right, and they are both wrong. Is a couple less destined to be together because they don't think of themselves that way? Is a couple *beshert* simply because they make that claim for themselves? And do we always choose our *beshert*, or do we sometimes flee in terror when we see our destiny embodied before us?

This much I do know: I have been alive for nearly sixty years, and I have tried to love many people, but it has only worked once, and I knew that it would the moment I met her. I could see our life stretching out together for all eternity, and so could she. Thirteen days later, I saw her again and I asked her to marry me. If I had had any courage at all, I would have asked her that very first night.

What is more astounding is that this relationship was clearly the beginning of my productive life. I had been floundering through life up till then, but suddenly I felt nurtured and enabled in a way that brought out all my most important talents and allowed me to express them. It opened the possibility for my becoming who I am, who I always was, who the world needed me to be. Could there have been more than one person I felt this way about? Could there have been more than one relationship that could have had this kind of impact on me? Theoretically, I suppose, it is possible. But the undeniable fact of my life is that there has been only one.

The same questions arise in relation to our vocation, our life's work. The idea of *shlichut,* or mission, the sense that everyone is called to this life in order to perform a unique and indispensable task, is deeply embedded in our tradition. There is a word that is enunciated by many important figures in the Torah at the moment in their lives when they are confronted by their destiny. It is the word *hineni.* Literally, it means "I am here," but as Rashi points out, the word has a far more complex range of meaning. *Hineni,* Rashi says, is the language of submission and preparedness. It is as if to say, I am prepared to live out my destiny. Moses says it at the burning bush, when he learns that it is his destiny to become the liberator of the people Israel. Abraham says it as he goes off to perform the *akedah,* the binding of his son Isaac. Joseph says it at the beginning of the long and torturous journey that will end with his saving the world from starvation and assuring the continuity of his own people. *Hineni.* I am prepared to live out my destiny. There are moments when each of us is called upon to utter this word. Sometimes we do and sometimes we don't.

Lawrence LeShan, a psychiatrist with whom I once trained during my tenure as a chaplain at Memorial Sloan-Kettering Hospital, had a controversial theory as to why people got cancer. He came to believe that many people became ill with cancer because they weren't expressing the meaning of their lives, because their unexpressed life force turned in on itself and began to devour the body that housed it. Many of the doctors at Sloan-Kettering resisted his ideas. They were afraid that if they were taken too literally they might lead patients to blame themselves for their illnesses. I could certainly understand this concern, but I also saw a kind of poetic if not literal truth to LeShan's ideas.

He told the story of one of his patients, a man in his sixties with a debilitating cancer. In working with this man, it became apparent to LeShan that he had always been terribly frustrated in his work. "What kind of work do you think would be more satisfying for you?" LeShan asked this man. "I'd like to be a doctor," the man replied. LeShan didn't know what to say at first. This man had never even been to college, and medical schools were not in the habit of accepting sixty-five-year-old applicants, regardless of their educational achievements. So LeShan probed further. "What is it that appeals to you about being a doctor?" he asked. "Well, I really love the idea of sitting in an office all day long and having people come to me with questions and being able to answer all their questions for them," the man said. Several years later, LeShan visited this man in Florida. He was working at a tourist information booth on one of Florida's busiest freeways. All day long he sat in the booth and people came to him with questions, and he was able to answer all their questions for them. He had been working at this job for several years. He was very happy, and his cancer had gone into remission.

LeShan had another patient who had been the leader of a major gang in New York City. But as time went on, all the gang members either died off or got married and went to work, and pretty soon there was no gang left to be the leader of. He came down with cancer shortly thereafter, and soon he wound up in LeShan's office. "What was it about being in a gang that you loved the most?" LeShan asked him. "It was the pace of the life, the rhythm of it," the ex–gang leader said. "There would be moments of terrific intensity when life and death were on the line, and then long, slow periods when we just sat around and savored those moments together. And then there was that sense of absolute trust that developed between you and the guys in your gang. If the guy in front of and the guy behind you didn't do exactly what they were supposed to do, you'd be dead, and that created such an incredible bond between us, such incredible trust. I've never felt that way about other people before or since."

The lightbulb went off in LeShan's mind right away. "You need to become a fireman," he said. This was easier said than done. The fire department was not in the habit of seeking out former gang leaders. But LeShan pulled a few strings, and he coached this guy through all the exams, and eventually he did become a fireman. He loved it even more than he had loved being a gang leader, and his cancer went into remission too. But ten years later he showed up in LeShan's office again. He had a terrible problem. He had turned out to be a terrific fireman. He had a ten-year record of distinguished service. He was so good, in fact, that they wanted to promote him to an office job. The pay was higher, the work was easier and completely safe. No one — not his boss, not his wife — could understand why he was so reluctant to accept the promotion. Nor could he explain to anyone but LeShan that he was terrified that if he stopped doing the work itself, if he stopped living by that rhythm and enjoying the bond that had developed between him and his fellow firefighters, he would come down with cancer again. I didn't train with LeShan for very long, so I never heard the end of this story, but I think about this guy all the time.

I never knew quite what to make of these stories and the dozens like them LeShan told. We all know people who seem to be living fulfilling lives yet are struck down by terrible illnesses anyway. The doctors at Sloan-Kettering were right to be concerned. One could easily misinterpret LeShan's stories as an attempt to blame the victim, to suggest that people who suffered from cancer had somehow brought it on themselves. Still I could never quite dismiss the feeling that there was at least a kernel of truth in what LeShan was saying. We are given certain tendencies by God — talents, abilities, predilections. And God really wants us to express these things. The world really needs us to do this. Our innate abilities are part of the infinite tapestry of being. We are necessary and inevitable creations, the bearers of unique and indispensable gifts. But neither God nor the world cares very much how we express these things. Neither God nor the world cares very much whether we express them as a doctor or as an information booth attendant, as a gang leader or as a fireman. The key question always becomes, what do we love to do? What activity makes us feel whole and flush with ourselves? When do we feel we are doing the thing that the world needs us to do?

Ralph Waldo Emerson said,

Everything in creation has its appointed painter or poet and remains in bondage like the princess in the fairy tale, until its appropriate liberator comes to set it free. The story of Sleeping Beauty is more than a fairy tale; it is an allegory of the life of every human being who fights his way through life.

But many of us lose this fight. Many of us never quite manage to do the thing we were clearly meant to do. Many of us hear the divine call but never manage to answer it, or never even permit ourselves to hear it to begin with. Not everyone finds his *beshert,* and not everyone finds his life's work. Many of us settle for a life partner who doesn't engage our deepest passion, and many of us settle for jobs we find neither fulfilling nor meaningful. Many of us simply lead the lives of quiet desperation Thoreau spoke about. Though everything is foreseen, free will is always in our hands. The people or the work we are destined for may very well present themselves to us, but we may choose not to accept them.

Why? The simplest answer to this question is fear. We are afraid of our lives, as afraid, perhaps, as we are of our deaths. In the book of Numbers there is a terrible story about the first time the Children of Israel came to the edge of the Promised Land and confronted their destiny head-on. This was at the very beginning of their wandering through the desert. They came to the border of the Promised Land and sent out scouts to help them prepare for their entry into Canaan. But the spies had a failure of nerve and they communicated their fear to the people, and the people refused to accept their destiny. They refused to go up into the land. As a consequence they were doomed to live out their lives in the wilderness in a meaningless meandering. Only their descendants would fulfill the life mission that had been intended for them.

I think that more often than not, we experience a failure in courage when confronted with our destiny. This is especially true in love. If we love deeply and passionately, we risk losing love. The person might not love us back, or even if they do, they might die. In fact they will certainly die, and then we will be faced with the agonizing pain of lost love. I saw this pain when my own father died. My mother and father did not lose their courage when confronted by their destiny together. They were both poor Depression kids without a penny in their pocket, but the first time they met, they knew they had to be together forever. They married when my mother was seventeen. My father was still in school and they were absolutely penniless. Everyone thought they were crazy, but they knew they had to be together, and they had a wonderful life, a meaningful and productive life that grew out of their love as surely as a lotus grows out of the mud. Then my father died and my mother was left on the other side of that love. It was unbearable for her. She fell into a mild depression for many years, and then developed Alzheimer's, a condition many in the family saw as a withdrawal from a world she no longer cared to live in.

I think there are many people who choose not to love out of fear of this kind of loss. If we love, we might lose love, and we may be afraid that this loss will be more than we can bear. When I first met my wife, I was a poet and a Zen student. I supported myself driving a Gray Line bus in San Francisco. The giant redwood forest in Muir Woods, at the foot of Mount Tamalpais, was our most popular destination. To get there we had to drive our forty-foot buses down a precipitous mountain road with one hairpin turn after another. We bus drivers fell into a dangerous game on that road. We came down it in caravans, daring each other to drive at increasingly reckless speeds, taking the hairpin turns blindly, veering dangerously close to the sheer drops by the side of the road, and all the while making macabre jokes to our white-knuckled, green-faced passengers. "Don't worry," we would call back to a terrified busload of tourists as we crashed hell-bent down the mountain, "the fainting spells have been coming far less frequently lately."

It was a tremendously foolish game, but it was great, exhilarating fun. The weirdest part was, I never felt a moment of fear as I barreled recklessly down that mountain with forty or fifty lives in my charge. It never occurred to me that anything could really happen, that anything could go wrong. Never, that is, until I met my wife. After that I was terrified every time I went down the mountain, always aware of how perilously close to going off the cliff I was. Suddenly I had something to lose. Suddenly my life had a kind of infinite value I had never felt it to have before. Suddenly I was aware of how much easier — how much less frightening — it was to live when one had nothing to lose, no love to risk losing. It's so much emptier too, but I'm afraid many people are quite willing to pay that price.

Is everyone who is alone guilty of a failure of courage? I rather doubt it. Love is a mystery of the first order, and I would be the last one to claim that I understood it enough to make such a charge. I think there must be all kinds of reasons why people find themselves alone, including bad luck. But this much I do know: love is our deepest need, and the fear of losing it prevents many of us from even trying to have it.

Yet I think there is an even deeper fear operating here than the fear of loss, and that is the fear of our own power. We get used to living without power and without love. We come to believe that this is how our lives should be. We become comfortable within the confines of these limitations. They surround us like the walls of a womb. When our real strength begins to declare itself, when the intensity of love presents itself to us, we are torn out of this comfortable cocoon. This is a frightening experience, and if our courage fails us, we will choose to live without our full power, without passionate intensity. We will settle for something that feels safer and more comfortable. Better to settle for a life that seems easier to hold.

I think we struggle with this same kind of failure of courage when confronted with the life's work we are destined to do. If we were to actually try to do the thing we were meant to do and we failed at it, what would be left of our life after that? Better to hold that great novel you've always felt inside you in potential, than to risk trying to actually write it. What if you failed? Then you wouldn't even have that potential novel anymore. You wouldn't have anything. Better to not try and to just hold on to the dream. At least you'd still have that.

We see Moses wrestling with all this at the burning bush, when God comes to tell him what his mission in life is to be. The book of Exodus is the story of the liberation of the Children of Israel, of the irrepressible movement of the Jewish people toward being — toward realization. But it is mirrored by a similar movement within Moses. When Moses encounters God at the burning bush, he encounters his own destiny as well. He experiences personal liberation. He discovers why it was that he came into this world. He becomes free to express his divine nature, to become what it is that he must become.

In this same scene, God tells Moses that his name is *ehiyeh asher ehiyeh* — "I am that I am," or "I will become what I will become." The will of God is expressed in the need of everything and everyone on earth to become what they are, what they are supposed to be.

If we dare to look, we can find the same impulse and the same struggle in our own heart as well. Few things are as frightening to us as a confrontation with our destiny, with the way God has made us.

Most of us react precisely the way Moses reacts when we feel that impulse to become what we were meant to be stirring within us. We resist.

Moses resists no less than five times, and his resistance is instructive. He has the same anxieties we all experience when confronted with the soul's need to express itself. First he says, "Who am I to do this thing?" The first obstacle in his liberation is that he doesn't believe in himself. I'm just a poor schmohawk. I'm not a fit vessel for the will of God. Then he says, "When I come to the Children of Israel they are going to ask me what is God's name? Who is this God in whose name you claim to be acting? But I don't know Your name so how can I claim to be acting in it?" Then he says, Well, even if I believe in myself, "they won't believe in me." I'm just a poor schmohawk. I'll look like an idiot. And then he says, "I'm no good at public speaking. [I'm just a poor schmohawk.] I have a clumsy mouth and a heavy tongue." And finally he says, "Send somebody else. Liberate these people by someone else's hand. [I'm just a poor schmohawk.] Whatever you do, don't send me!"

This is a pretty precise picture of how each of us reacts when confronted by the image of the divine within us struggling to come into this world. (1) We don't believe in ourselves. We don't believe we're important enough to have a divine mission. (2) We don't believe we are connected to God or that God has empowered us to be what we must be. (3) We don't believe others will believe in us. We are afraid of appearing foolish. (4) We don't believe we are adequate to the task. We don't believe we are capable of the mission God has given us. (5) We don't believe we are unique. We don't believe that we have anything special to offer. We see ourselves as a replaceable part. This is how it is that so many of us come to live twilit lives, bound lives, lives without meaning.

Emerson was right. Everything in creation does in fact remain in bondage until its appropriate liberator comes to set it free. What usually eludes us is the fact that the first thing we need to be liberated from is our own fear, our own sense of inadequacy. This liberation may be the most significant transformation we will ever face. Will we become the person we were meant to be? All other questions pale next to this one. We may catch a glimpse of who we really are and what our divine mission really is. This may be very different from who we think we are or from the sense of inadequacy we have absorbed from the people around us. We may confront our fear for the paper tiger it is. We might just decide to walk through our fear and come out the other side.

Everything is foreseen, and free will is always in our hands. God implants tendencies — unique and indispensable abilities — in our minds, hearts, bodies, and souls. We may choose to use them or not. Even before that, we may choose to see them or not.

God gives us someone to love. We may choose to love them, or love may be too frightening for us and we may choose partners it is impossible for us to love, or people who are incapable of loving us back. Then we'll be safe. Then we won't have risked anything — except, of course, our lives. Then we won't have to hold anything, either power or passion, that feels like more than we are used to holding, more than we are comfortable holding.

It's a frightening thing to think that the world depends on our becoming who we are, and it is even more frightening to feel the power of that. Don't run away from that fear. Collect yourself and stand up to it. The reality is that you can hold it. You must hold it. See this and be deeply still. Let the secret of who you are and how you love arise out of this stillness. Like all things that arise out of stillness, they come from God.

PRACTICE POINTS

A Five-Step Antidote for Panic

The five-step program Moses and God proposed together at the edge of the Red Sea is not just an exercise in theology. At its base it is a very practical program for meeting those times in life when we know we have to do something but have no idea what to do, those moments of panic when we feel life pressing in on us without presenting us with either a safe escape route or a reasonable alternative. Time and time again, I have urged this program on people who find themselves in such circumstances, and I have found that it works. It works in both macro- and microcosm. We can use this to come to terms with the various impossibilities in our lives over a long period of time, but it also works for short-term emergencies.

We find ourselves in a terrible dilemma and we are appropriately frightened. We know something must be done, but we have no idea what to do and this terrifies us. So (1) *al tira-u* — we stop running away from our fear, we stop letting our fear push us around. We say to ourselves, I feel frightened now, but I have faith that there is nothing to be frightened of, that the calamities I imagine might happen are just that — just products of my overly fertile imagination.

Then (2) *hityatzvu* — we make a stand, we stand still, we reconstruct ourselves, we collect our awareness, we bring it in from the many corners of mind where it has scattered in its terror; we let go of our terror and we allow the world to reconstitute itself. We can do this in meditation, bringing our awareness out of the peripheral corners of mind and into the center with the momentum of the in-breath, or we can do it wherever we happen to be, whenever this kind of panic arises, simply closing our eyes for a moment and reconstituting ourselves, drawing our awareness into the center as we breath in.

Then (3) *uru* — we see our experience for what it really is. Collected and free of panic, the mind perceives our experience with clarity. It sees what is, the moment that has just come into being and not some fearful product of our panic and our imagination.

Then (4) *tacharishun* — we come to the point of stillness. When we are flush with our experience, a wonderful stillness ensues. It is a reflection of our stillness of mind, a stillness that comes when the mind is no longer being pulled back and forth between what is and what we imagine.

So we have stopped panicking, we have gathered ourselves together, we have brought our awareness in from all the corners where it has scattered itself out of fear, and we have allowed the new moment to construct itself. As a consequence, we have seen it precisely for what it is. A deep stillness has ensued from this open-eyed inhabiting of the present moment, this sense of being flush with our experience.

Finally, the next action — the necessary action, the inevitable action — arises out of this stillness of its own accord, and (5) *v'yisau* — we move forward, not really acting of ourselves, but giving ourselves to the action the moment requires.

We can practice these steps over time, addressing a larger

question in our life that has us stumped — What should I do about this relationship? Should I quit this job and look for another? — or we can practice them in moments of panic as they arise. We can practice them in meditation, or we can practice them in the midst of our lives, as we go along the way.

Expanding Our Boundaries

Fear that is not the product of an imagined phantom is often caused by the sense that we are suddenly in possession of more energy than we are used to, than we know how to handle. We don't feel large enough, strong enough to hold it. This energy is a new strength announcing itself, and if we shy away from it out of fear, we will never grow into the people we need to be, we will never become who we truly are. One way to work with this fear is to expand our sense of mental and spiritual boundaries. Often we are afraid of a new strength because we feel we are too small for it, that we don't have room to hold it. We feel as if we might explode from it. But the truth is, we literally have all the room in the world. The soul knows no boundaries.

Sitting in meditation, we can experience this boundlessness. Turning our attention from the breath and the body to the mind, we see that we are sitting in a boundless field, a sea without limit. Thoughts, feelings, impulses rise up on this sea like waves, but the sea itself has no boundaries except those we have imposed on it. Even as we imagine ourselves to be in a limitless field, nevertheless, there is a vague sense of edge to this field. Breathing out, we let go of this boundary. Breathing in, we find ourselves inhabiting an expanded field of mind. Breathing out again, we let go again, and the boundary expands still further. This is a very good exercise for dealing with *norah*, that chilling fear that comes over us when we begin to glimpse our real strength. And it is an exercise we can do in formal meditation or in the midst of our lives whenever we are overcome by this kind of fear. Letting go of the edges of our consciousness as we breathe out, we make the mind larger and more comfortable in holding our full strength.

Chapter Five

Sacred Emptiness

1. The Emptiness at the Center

Rabbi Eleazar got it right. All this perfection is indeed fading into the earth. One feels this quite acutely around the Jewish High Holidays, when many more people than usual seem to die. This is not convenient for a rabbi, of course. The High Holidays are our busy season, like tax time for accountants, and there's nothing like a funeral for throwing one's entire schedule out of whack. Whole afternoons have to be canceled. That quiet time you set aside to finally get down to work on your sermons is consumed in a single gulp. I was complaining about this publicly at a board meeting one year, the Monday night before Rosh Hashanah. There had been even more deaths than usual this

High Holiday season and I was feeling swamped. The next day, Tuesday, September 11, 2001, brought a storm tide of death six days before Rosh Hashanah. I was holding special services, doing grief counseling, and conducting funerals almost up until the minute the holidays began. The last funeral was for a woman I had only known for twenty minutes. Yet I stood over her grave weeping. Perhaps precisely because I didn't know her very well, I had permitted her death to stand for all these other deaths in my heart, all the impermanence that the past week had brought so relentlessly into focus.

I had met this woman on my way back from one of the many funerals I had had to do early in the week. She lived in Colma, the little town just outside San Francisco where all the cemeteries are. I thought I could kill two birds with one stone, as they say. She was dying herself, and I had promised her hospice worker that I would try to make a visit if I could in these last days of her life. When the hospice worker called to make this request, she told me that this woman had been asking to see a rabbi. When I told her how busy rabbis were at this time of year, she had pulled out a trump card that always works on me. She said she had heard a lot about me and she thought I was the only one who might be able to reach this woman. Give me some basis for pretending that I am indispensable and I will do anything for you.

So on the way back from the funeral, I tried to call this woman repeatedly on my cell phone, but the number I had been given was continuously busy, and finally I decided to just go and try to see her.

She lived in an apartment house in a poor neighborhood in the Outer Mission. Her caretaker, a young Filipino, led me back to her bedroom. There I encountered a shocking apparition: a skeleton in a fetching pink satin nightgown, facedown in bed. As I moved around the bed, I could see that this skeleton was alive and was, in fact, writing very slowly, laboriously, on a pad. She was clutching two things very close to her chest, a respirator and a pack of cigarettes. With a white, bony hand she motioned for me to take a seat on the portable toilet next to her bed. When she was finished writing, she said, "Rub my back." These were her first words to me, not even so much as a hello.

"I used to take morphine for the pain," she said, "but the back rubs work much better."

I stood beside the bed and tried to comply. It was hard to find a place to rub. Her backbone was a plate of sheer bone with ridges on the spine like jagged rocks. Finally I found some softness near her neck and started to rub there. "I like that," she said.

She had a question she wanted to ask me. It seems that some Seventh-Day Adventists had been coming to read the Bible to her every day. She worried that it wasn't right for her to have them there, but they gave great back rubs.

"Are you worried that they're going to convert you?" I asked.

"No," she said. "I'm not very religious, but I'm Jewish to the bone, and nothing's ever going to change that."

"Then just enjoy the back rubs and listen to the Bible as if it were music," I said.

"Yes," she said. "Everything's music."

She told me she was paranoid of her caretakers. The soap they used on her gave her a rash. She kept telling them that, but they kept on using the same soap anyway. She thought they were doing it on purpose, and she thought they were screwing with her telephones too. Her regular phone no longer worked (that explained why I hadn't been able to reach her before), and now she was afraid they were going to take her cell phone away too. She was clutching a cell phone to her chest as we spoke. I wondered if there was any basis for her suspicions, or if it was just what often happens when your life is utterly dependent on others and you worry whether they are caring for you properly.

I asked her if there were any other questions she wanted to ask me.

"Yes," she said. "Will you bury me?"

"Sure," I said.

"Well, how much do you charge?" she said.

I told her my usual fee, but I said I realized she probably didn't have it and I'd be happy to bury her for nothing.

No, she said. She insisted she wanted to pay me.

"Well, I'll do it for one dollar in that case," I said.

"How about ten," she said.

"You drive a hard bargain," I said.

"I love you," she said.

"I love you too," I said.

"No you don't," she said.

"How can you doubt that I love you when I just agreed to bury you for ten bucks?" I said. "Would you like me to say the Vidui" — the traditional deathbed confession — "for you?"

"What does it say?" she wanted to know.

I read her the Vidui in English, secretly believing that I was tricking her, that this English reading would count as her deathbed confession whether she wanted me to repeat it in Hebrew or not.

So I read the part where it says that she acknowledged that her life was in God's hands, and in the unlikely event that God decided to heal her, that would be very nice, but if God was bound to take her, let God take her in his hands with love, and let her death be an atonement for all her sins, and let God protect all the loved ones she left behind whose souls were bound up with her soul.

"Oh yes, say it," she said. "Say those words." So I said them again, this time in Hebrew.

After that I could tell by the look of exhaustion on her face that while she had been very happy to have me there, she would be even happier if I would now leave.

"Good-bye," she said, with considerable effort and feeling.

"Good-bye," I said, and I realized that I would never see her again.

Outside in the living room, I spoke to the attendant. I told him about the soap. I told him about the telephones. He said he knew about the phone. He had tried to use the cell phone to call to get the regular phone fixed, but she wouldn't let him have the cell phone. He was clearly a lovely man. I asked him his name. "Elijah," he said. "Like the prophet."

A few days later I stood over her grave weeping. Was it because she had somehow managed to insinuate herself into my soul, to become a part of me, in the course of that brief twenty minutes? Or was I weeping because to meet someone only at the moment of their leaving life was an unbearable reminder of the impermanence of all life, of all things, in a week so scarred by impermanence, in a week when death had erupted into the midst of life so rudely at Ground Zero.

All that week I had been beset by the disquieting intuition that life would never be the same again, that the fall of the twin towers had permanently altered not only the skyline of Manhattan but the American psyche as well. Many people expressed that feeling then — television commentators, the people one spoke to on the street. Now it is several years later, and it seems clear that we all were right. Americans are much less prone to act like immortals these days. We seem much more aware of our contingency, our impermanence. We are finding it considerably more difficult to live in denial of death, the yawning void that awaits us at the end. Is this necessarily a bad thing? It is if we rely on our usual stratagems for dealing with uncertainty: holding on to the familiar for dear life, resisting change with everything we have, allowing ourselves to be dominated by fear and suspicion. But there is another way of dealing with the grim realities the events of recent years have thrust in our faces, and that is to make friends with the emptiness at the core of our being, to come to know it, to become comfortable with it, to come to understand it as the gateway to an enduring flow of being, beyond impermanence and beyond death.

•

Hanukkah is a lovely little holiday but one greatly inflated in importance in the West because of its proximity to Christmas. In fact, although Hanukkah is a Talmudic rather than a biblical holiday, there was a time when the rabbis of the Talmud resisted its celebration and tried to deny it a place on the sacred calendar. We see remnants of this resistance in the scant attention Hanukkah receives in both the Bible and the Talmud. In fact, it receives no attention in the Hebrew Bible at all. The rabbis effaced the book of the Maccabees from the biblical canon altogether. The only reason we still know it at all is because our good friends the Catholics preserved it in theirs. And whereas every other Jewish holiday has an entire tractate of the Talmud devoted to it, Hanukkah only merits a few pages of a tractate otherwise devoted to Shabbat.

Why did the rabbis resist Hanukkah so? There are many theories about this. First of all, virtually every culture in human history has celebrated a festival of light at the darkest time of the year — the winter solstice — and the rabbis were probably not thrilled about incorporating a rite with such obviously pagan origins into the Jewish sacred calendar. Nor was there any great love lost between the rabbis and the Hasmoneans — the dynastic descendants of the Maccabees whose rule over Israel was characterized by imperialism, tyranny, and the corruption of the Temple cult. In fact, the rabbis of the Talmud were originally a band of proto-beatniks who rose up in rebellion against the Hasmoneans and proposed a religious program of prayer and study as an alternative to the corrupt sacrificial worship over which the Hasmonean priests presided at the Great Temple in Jerusalem.

Nor did the rabbis love the book of the Maccabees itself. They regarded it as insufficiently religious. God never appears in it, and no miracles are performed, except of course for the rather prosaic miracle of a small number of Maccabean upstarts prevailing over the great Syrian Hellenist armies of the day; but this is not so much a miracle as an upset, the sort of thing one might see in the National Football League on any given Sunday. It is a rather bloodthirsty book as well, one that glories in military prowess and armed insurrection.

But the people loved this book, and they were absolutely determined to have a celebration of light at the winter solstice, when the world was frighteningly, depressingly dark. So the rabbis gave in, albeit grudgingly. They devoted a scant paragraph of the Talmud to a brief rewrite of the end of the biblical story, one that added a miracle by God to the historical account of the book of the Maccabees, and declared a holiday, a festival of light at the time of the winter solstice, to celebrate this miracle. The miracle, of course, is the miracle of the oil that burned for eight days. There is no mention of this in the Bible, which merely describes in rather prosaic terms the restoration and rededication of the Temple (the word *Hanukkah* means "dedication") after the Maccabees had recaptured it from the Hellenist hordes. The courtyards are cleaned and repaired, great stones are hewn, and a menorah is certainly lit, but nothing supernatural occurs. In the Talmudic rewrite, however, we read the following:

> What is the reason for the celebration of Hanukkah? When the Greeks captured the Temple, they defiled all the oils in it. When the Hasmonean warriors defeated them [and recaptured the Temple], they searched, but they could only find one jar of oil which had the seal of the high priest on it [and was therefore fit for burning in the Great Temple], and this jar did not have enough oil in it except for one day's burning. But a miracle occurred; they lit the lamp and the oil burned from this one jar for eight days. In the following years, these days were fixed and made into holidays.

Neatly and cleanly, the rabbis of the Talmud have solved a number of problems at once with this story. First of all, it fits rather nicely with a solstice celebration. The miracle it adds to the lore of Hanukkah is precisely a miracle of light. And above all, it's a miracle! Now we can have an authentic Jewish celebration. Now we can sing Hallel, the special psalms of praise with which we always commemorate miracles on our holidays. And the math works out perfectly too. It took eight days to dedicate a temple — we saw this when Moses dedicated the Tabernacle in the Wilderness, when Solomon dedicated the Great Temple of Jerusalem, and when the Second Temple was rebuilt and rededicated in the time of Ezra and Nehemiah. Now we have eight days of miracles as well — one day of the holiday for each miracle. Perfect.

Well, not so fast. If we think about it, we really only have seven days of miracles here. After all, according to the Talmud, "this jar did not have enough oil in it except for one day's burning," but one day's burning it had. So if the oil from this jar burned for eight days, we only have seven days of miracles. The first day was not a miracle; it was just the jar's contents burning as they ought to have burned, without any help from the supernatural.

Now this discrepancy may not bother you very much, and to tell you the truth, I'm not sure it bothers me either, but it really bugged the rabbis, and particularly the classical commentators on the Talmud. They tried to wriggle out of this one for a couple of thousand years. If you were going to have eight days of holiday, you needed eight days of miracles. So according to one commentator, the Hasmoneans must have divided the oil in the jar into eight equal portions, and even though each night's portion only had a few hours of oil to burn, the lamp burned miraculously all night long for each of the eight nights. Ergo, eight nights of miracles instead of seven.

But others pointed out that this violated a clear principle of Jewish law, i.e., one should never pass up the sure opportunity to perform a mitzvah — a commandment — even though there was a chance that one would be able to fulfill even more commandments as a result. If you had enough oil to fulfill one night's commandment — to burn the lamp for one night — then you were enjoined to burn it and let God take care of the other nights as God saw fit.

Other commentators said that after they had filled the menorah lamp with the proper measure of oil from the jar, the jar remained full as in the beginning (or alternatively, that the lamp itself was still full of oil after burning all night), but this solution merely shifted the problem from the first day to the last. It was like a Rubik's Cube. There were still only seven days of miracles.

It wasn't until the late twentieth century that the great modern Talmud scholar Shaul Lieberman located an ancient manuscript of the Talmud that seemed to solve this conundrum that had baffled the commentators for so long. The critical line in the Talmud, remember, read "this jar did not have enough oil in it except for one day's burning." The English word "except" is a loose translation of the Hebrew *eleh*, which means "but" or "except." This word is often abbreviated in the Talmud by the letter *aleph* with a little pipchick (') after it, and so it is here in most of the Talmudic manuscripts that have come down to our hands. Or so it seems. But Lieberman found an older manuscript of the Talmud in which the critical word is not abbreviated but rather spelled out in full, and lo and behold, it is not the word *eleh* after all but rather *afilu*, another word beginning with the letter *aleph* but which means not "except" but "even." Apparently this was the original version of the text: "This jar did not have enough oil in it *even* for one day's burning." There was virtually no oil in the jar at all! Now the problem disappears. There was not enough oil for even one day, therefore we have eight days of miracles and we're all set.

But this is more than a semantic change. This is a theological change as well. Now the meaning of the miracle is entirely different. Before, the miracle was that the light burned against great odds, longer than we could have had any reason to expect it to burn. Now the miracle is that the light flared up at all. This is a miracle different in both quantity and kind from the one we imagined we were celebrating all those centuries. This is not the miracle of overcoming impossible odds, this is the miracle of the world arising out of emptiness, out of nothing.

This, in fact, is the primal miracle, the first story the Torah chooses to tell us.

In the beginning, God created the heavens and the earth. The earth was unformed and void, and darkness was on the face of the deep. And the Spirit of God hovered over the face of the waters, and God said "Let there be light," and there was light.

In the beginning, there was nothing, a primal emptiness, a formless chaos, a darkness layered over a deep void. Then the spirit (*ruach*) of God, itself an emptiness (the word *ruach* also means "wind," an empty movement, an effect that lacks substance of its own and can only be seen in the things it passes through, in the trees and the fields and the sea), hovered over this void and called light into being out of this nothingness.

We are not the first to connect these two lights — the primordial light of creation and the Hanukkah light. The rabbis of the Kabala, the Jewish mystical tradition, claimed that these lights were one and the same, that the light we contemplate on Hanukkah is in fact the Or Genuzah (literally, "the light that was stored away"), the primordial light of creation which had arisen out of nothing.

This light is not the light that illuminates the world. That light was created on the fourth day, when God made the sun to light the day and the moon to light the night. No, this primordial light, this Or Genuzah, is the light out of which everything is made, the constituent element of all reality, the radiant emptiness at the center of all being, an emptiness that itself was called up by God out of emptiness.

As we mentioned earlier, the Kabala teaches that before the universe was created, God existed as the Ain Sof, the endlessness, God's essential emptiness, powerful and without form or attribute. This was such a powerful emptiness that nothing could coexist with it, so in order to create the universe, God had to remove the better part of his light from a tiny spot at the center of the Ain Sof. This tiny dot became the entire known universe. Lines of force run down from the Ain Sof through the world of *atzilut* (pure spiritual emanation), to the world of *briyah* (conception), to the world of *yetzirah* (formation), to this world of *asiyah,* the world of activity and physicality. Here, many steps removed from the supernal emptiness that gave us life, we are largely unaware of that emptiness. We are mesmerized by the appearance of things, by the stuff and matter by which we imagine ourselves to be surrounded.

But we don't completely buy it. Deep down, we don't quite believe in it. Something in us still senses the Ain Sof. Something in us intuits the emptiness of all things. We need to be something, but we can't quite escape the terrifying suspicion that really we might be nothing. We want the world to have substance, but something in us knows that at bottom, even the hardest matter is just light, a radiant emptiness. We behave as though we believe in the hardness of objects — of tables and dressers and chairs. But when we close our eyes and pay close attention and press our hand into these things, they seem soft; there is a surprising give to them, as if they were made of plush velvet. Because the molecules of the hardwood tabletop are moving faster than the molecules of our hand, our hand doesn't fall right through to the floor, but rather stops at the surface of the table. So it is that we come to believe in its hardness; that it is, in fact, a thing. It is not. It is made of light. It is empty. It is a radiant nothingness.

And something in us senses the inadequacy of all the language we use to clothe the nakedness of our experience. Every time we say something, we realize that it isn't completely true. At the base of our experience is an emptiness, a powerful void without qualities or characteristics, without form or substance, so that anything we might say about our lives ends up feeling like an inauthentic imposition, an overlay on reality. Like the invisible man wrapping himself in bandages so that he can be seen, we are constantly covering over this void with nouns and adjectives, but none of them really adheres. None of them is finally persuasive. We give our life a narrative, we tell ourselves a story about it, and it seems to hold up a good deal of the time, but not all of the time. Fragments of our life that just don't fit the story keep popping up, and we keep trying to push them down again so that the story can remain intact. But all this pushing down and propping up and laying over consumes a good deal of our energy, more of it than we can afford.

The Tabernacle in the Wilderness and its spiritual descendant, the Great Temple of Jerusalem, were inverse images of the Ain Sof. The Ain Sof was a charged emptiness surrounding the universe, working its way down in concentric spirals to the world of matter and action at its center.

Both the Temple and the Tabernacle were elaborate structures, a complex mass of stuff arranged in intricate concentric patterning around a charged emptiness at the center. The Holy of Holies, the sacred space at the center of the sanctuary, was essentially a vacated space, a place no one could ever enter except the high priest, and even he for only a few moments on Yom Kippur.

Like the Ain Sof, the emptiness at the center of the Holy of Holies was so powerfully charged that nothing could coexist with it. That's why no one could enter that space. When Nadav and Avihu, the two sons of Aaron the high priest, drew too near to the Holy of Holies without being authorized to do so, their souls were immediately and utterly consumed by a devouring flame.

The Torah devotes five weekly readings — fully half the book of Exodus — to a highly detailed, highly repetitive description of the architecture of the Tabernacle in the Wilderness. The classical commentators make a few lame allegorical interpretations of this material and then fall silent in the face of it. Their silence attests to the point of all this architecture; the purpose of the Tabernacle was not to *mean,* but to *be.* The Tabernacle didn't symbolize anything; rather the Tabernacle's form itself communicated important spiritual principles, and the Torah takes great pains to engrave the image of this form on our psyches.

The Tabernacle, for example, is consistently constructed out of many things joined to become one thing. The roof consists of many small cloths joined to become one great curtain, and the walls are made of many small boards joined into one. Is this a metaphor for human community? The Torah seems to suggest as much by using the phrase "a woman to her sister" to describe the joining of the curtains and the boards to one another. It is if the Tabernacle were trying to tell us, "You are not just you. Shift the focus of your life away from your ego. The true meaning of your life is not your discrete identity, your self, but rather, those points where you intersect with others, where you become part of a flow of being, a community."

But there is the suggestion that something larger is being intimated here as well — the interpenetrating, interconnected nature of

all things, of the universe itself. And both these themes are rein-
forced by a second architectural principle that the Tabernacle consistently follows, to wit: the points of juncture are always given
greater value and importance than the objects being joined themselves. If the boards are made of wood, they are joined by silver
sockets. If they are made of silver, they are joined by gold. Like an
Escher print, the Tabernacle seeks to shift our spiritual focus from
the hard objects of the world to the spaces between them, to the
nexus points. And it wants to create an inward momentum as well.
The closer we get to the center of the Tabernacle, the more valuable
the building materials become. There is cloth on the perimeter, then
wood, then silver, and finally, at the sacred center, only gold.

But by far the most striking structural characteristic of the
Tabernacle is its concentric form. The Tabernacle is a highly
centered affair. There are layers upon layers of surrounding curtains, like the skins of an onion. And inside, there are courtyards
within courtyards within courtyards, all of them focusing us on —
pulling us into — the empty space at the center, the vacated space,
the Holy of Holies.

This architectural feature seems to have been borrowed from
a standard ancient Near Eastern sacred structure, the ziggurat.
The ziggurat was a God-catching machine. It used a powerful
inward, concentric momentum and a vacuum at the center to lure
the gods in as if it were trapping them. I know how this works.
When I was a kid I used to love to play ski ball on the boardwalk
at Coney Island. In ski ball, you rolled a small metal ball down a
long wooden alley that sloped up at the end toward a seven-ringed
black-and-white target. If the ball hopped up into the outermost
layer of the target, you got a small number of points, and if it went
into the center, you got the most. I was very good at ski ball,

because I soon discovered that the concentricity of the target and the hole at the center of it created a momentum that seemed to pull the ball into the bull's-eye as if of its own accord if you could only get yourself out of the way.

So it was that the presence of God seemed to be drawn into the center of the Tabernacle by all this concentricity and by the emptiness at the center. Only it wasn't a trap. It was all God's idea in the first place, and it was such a powerful idea that it suffused the entire Torah and became a hallmark of the encounter between God and humanity. When God speaks to human beings, the speech often takes the form of a chiasmus — the first idea matching the last idea, the language of the second line matching the language of the second to last line, and the essential message of the speech lying at the center. Examine, for example, the following speech that God makes to Moses toward the beginning of the book of Exodus.

I Am Adonai.   [A]

And I appeared to Abraham, Isaac, and Jacob as
El Shaddai, but by my name Adonai I did not
Make myself known to them.   [B]

And I have also established my covenant with them
To give them the land of Canaan, the land of their
Sojourning in which they were strangers.   [C]

And I have also heard the groaning of the children of
Israel whom the Egyptians kept in bondage
And I have remembered my covenant.   [D]

Therefore say to the Children of Israel
I Am Adonai
And I will release you from the burdens of Egypt
And deliver you from their bondage and redeem you
With outstretched arm and with great judgments.

And I will take you to be my people and I will be your God,
And you will know that I am Adonai your God
Who releases you from the burdens of Egypt.   [D]

And I will bring you to the land which I swore
I would lift my hand to give   [C]

To Abraham, Isaac, and Jacob, and I will give it to you
For a heritage.   [B]

I Am Adonai.   [A]

Like the Holy of Holies at the center of the tabernacle, God's essential message — the promise of redemption from Egypt (in italics here) — is enfolded in a concentric structure. The first and last verses (A) are identical: *I Am Adonai.* The three patriarchs, Abraham, Isaac, and Jacob, are the subject of the second and second to last verses (B); the Promised Land is the subject of the third and third to last verses (C); and the release from bondage is the subject of the fourth and fourth to last verses (D). The chiasmus expresses perfect balance and harmony, qualities appropriate to the speech of God.

It also expresses love, which is why the Italian sonnet, the earliest sonnet form, was always written as a chiasmus. Here, for instance, is a Petrarchan sonnet by Sir Thomas Wyatt that uses a deer hunt as a metaphor for courtly love.

Who so lists to hunt, I know where is an hind,   [A]
   But as for me, alas, I may no more   [B]
   The vain travail hath wearied me so sore.   [B]
I am of them that farthest cometh behind;   [A]
Yet may I by no means my wearied mind   [A]
    Draw from the deer: but as she fleeth afore,   [B]
    Fainting I follow. I leave off therefore,   [B]
Since in a net I seek to hold the wind.   [A]

So read the first two quatrains of this sonnet. The rhyme scheme encloses itself. As in the passage from Exodus, the first and last rhyme is also found in the center and encloses and is enclosed by the second rhyme. Perfect harmony. Complete embrace.

Even the Torah has a chiasmic structure. The Torah has five books. Five itself, five marks or digits (| | | | |), is a chiasmus: two parallel outer layers, two inner layers, and a single digit at the center. The middle book of the five books of the Torah, the book of Leviticus, the instruction manual for the priests, takes place entirely in the Tabernacle. At the center of the book of Leviticus, in Parshat Shemini, there is an oversized letter *vuv* in the word *gachon,* or belly. This enlarged *vuv* marks the exact geographical center — the belly, as it were — of the Torah. There are precisely as many letters after this *vuv* in the Torah as there are before it. And Parshat Shemini takes place at the exact center of the Tabernacle — at the Holy of Holies. As the *parsha* begins, the Tabernacle has been erected exactly as God has instructed, the sacrifices have been made, the priests have been anointed, and the Tabernacle has been dedicated. And precisely as God has promised, when all this has been done God appears as a visible flame on the altar just outside the Holy of Holies. The people are astounded. They fall on their faces and prostrate themselves to God.

Then disaster strikes. Two of Aaron's sons, Nadav and Avihu, rush forward in their excitement, make an unauthorized approach to the Holy of Holies, offer unsanctioned incense, and are immediately consumed by fire themselves. But this is a strange fire. It consumes their souls but leaves their bodies intact.

There are many such chiasmic arrangements in the Torah, and curiously, this is what we always find at their sacred center, the appearance of God coupled with calamity — failure and death. As I mentioned earlier, the Torah devotes five weekly Torah portions to its description of the highly concentric Tabernacle, and the number five is itself a chiasmus. But this five-week compilation of architectural detail and repetition is interrupted exactly in the middle by the story of the golden calf, a story that features both calamity and a powerful appearance by God. So even the literary rendering of the architectural details of the Tabernacle reflects this curious concentricity — layers upon layers of stuff, surrounding an appearance of the Infinite, and the specter of death.

You find this even if you turn the Torah inside out and make it into a Möbius strip with its beginning and its end at the center. The Torah has no real beginning or end anyway. We read it continuously in a cycle, ending and beginning again on the same day, the holiday called Simchat Torah. The first letter of the Torah is the *veit* (V or B) of the word *Breshit* — "In the beginning." The last letter of the Torah is the *lamed* (L) of the word *Yisrael*. The letters *lamed veit* spell the word *lev*, "heart" or "center." So the beginning and the end of the Torah are quite literally its center. God appears in the beginning of the Torah — in fact that's all there is there — and God appears at the end of the Torah as well, in the ringing words of *Ha'azinu,* the Torah's final prophecy, and in the farewell kiss God plants on Moses's lips as he lies dying in the Torah's final scene. And there is calamity at the beginning and the end of the Torah as well. There is the fall from Eden at the beginning, the very beginning of failure and death, and there are both the tragic nature of the Torah's final prophecy and the tragic death of Moses at the end of the Torah.

So from beginning to end, and especially at its center, the Torah continuously expresses this formal pattern, an elaborate structure, carefully centered around both the infinite and the impermanent, around God and death, around change and that which is beyond change; in short, around the great flow of being that is God's very name.

2. No Stopping Place

What all this means to convey is that God and death are inextricably linked. God is truth, and the truth of our lives includes death and emptiness, impermanence and suffering. The truth is that our lives are a constant flow utterly devoid of stopping places. Our lives rise up and then fall away every moment. We are disposed to like the rising up and to fear the falling away, which reeks of the emptiness we are trying to deny at all costs. So we try to hold on to the last moment that arose, to stop it from falling away, and in doing so, we cause the flow to spasm, and the force of the next moment wanting to arise manifests itself to us as pain and suffering.

I have been struggling with a back problem for most of my adult life, a disk in the lower back that herniates periodically. Recently I started seeing a new doctor, who explained to me that while the body may seem solid and fixed, it is really constantly in flux, always trying to strike a balance between stability and flexibility. We are poorly balanced creatures, she explained, especially since we have been standing on two legs, a very meager and spindly base for the mass of our body. We would be much better off if we had a big tail like a kangaroo, a broad third leg to help us balance. But we don't have a tail, so stability is always a precarious undertaking for us. If there is a problem with one of our legs — a bum knee or a turned ankle — the rest of the body tries to compensate for the resulting instability, usually with unfortunate results. I've had a bad left knee in recent years, and it threw my balance out of whack, making my legs an even more undependable base than usual. The disk in my spine was quite well intentioned, my doctor explained. It was only trying to help out, only attempting to compensate for this new instability in my left leg by thrusting itself to the right. It didn't mean to hurl itself out of my spinal column altogether, but that's what happened.

I admired my doctor's effort to raise the pain in my back to the level of a universal truth. We experience the world we live in as a fixed and solid place, but really it is empty of substance, constantly in flux, constantly striving for a point of balance it can never completely attain. The Jewish sacred calendar reflects this reality. It is a long dance in which fullness is always giving way to decline, and decline to fullness. I feel this most poignantly in the summer months, the time of fullness — the longest days of the year, the time when the trees are most full of sap and the sun is the warmest. In the Jewish calendar this is the time we begin to move from fullness to decline. We commemorate revelation at Shavuot in the late spring; this is a high point, when we receive the Torah — our seminal idea — from God Almighty on a mountain-top. And the next moment, decline sets in. We begin to move toward Tisha B'Av and its dark themes of exile and the destruction of the Temple.

There is a weird holiday called Tu B'Av — the fifteenth day of Av — largely unknown and uncelebrated in modern times. According to the Mishnah, there was no happier day in the year than the fifteenth of Av, when virgins just past marriageable age went forth dressed all in white to dance in the vineyards and to challenge the young men of Israel to take them as brides though they might not be either the youngest nor the most beautiful women in the world. The image of these unmarried women just past their prime, dancing, dressed in white, just a little overripe and a little desperate is a pretty accurate metaphor for this season of the year — for the moment of fullness, after which less and less sap is found in the trees, and less and less light in the days. Fullness inevitably gives way to decline. Revelation gives way to the collapse of all ideas from the weight of their own limitations. Every house is built up and then inevitably, it falls, and a new house arises in its stead.

So in the summer, in the fullness of the year, the sacred calendar concerns itself with emptiness and collapse. Fullness and decline are intimately linked. The end of one is the beginning of the other. When the moment of fullness comes, we begin to turn toward decline. Conversely, decline and destruction necessarily precede renewal; a tearing down is necessary before rebuilding is possible. Winter gives way to spring. Dead branches fall to the floor of the forest and become part of the loam beneath it, and then new life rises up out of this dead matter. The father dies so that the son can finally become fully a man.

And all these things — fullness, decline, destruction, renewal, tearing down, rebuilding — are actually part of the same process, points on a single continuum, consecutive segments of a never-ending circle.

The year builds itself up and then it begins to let go of itself. The natural cycle of the cosmos, the rise and fall, the impermanence and the continuity, all express themselves in this turning. The walls come down and suddenly we can see, suddenly we recognize the nature of our estrangement from God, and this recognition is the beginning of our reconciliation with God.

We spoke earlier of how the Torah painstakingly engraves the image of the Tabernacle and its sacred structure in our psyches. It has occurred to me in recent years that the Jewish calendar year does the same thing with another image, the image of the fall of the Temple, the image of its walls falling down, its destruction and our exile. The calendar year engraves this image in our psyches through a series of public fasts. On the fifteenth of Tevet, which falls in late November and December, we fast in memory of the beginning of the siege of Jerusalem. On the seventeenth of Tammuz, a midsummer month, we fast in memory of the breach of the city's walls toward the end of this siege. Exactly three weeks later, on the ninth of Av (Tisha B'Av), we observe a major fast — the longest and most difficult fast of the year — to remember the fall of Jerusalem and the destruction of the Temple. Then seven weeks later, on the day after Rosh Hashanah, we observe the Fast of Gedalyah. Gedalyah was the Jewish governor who presided over Israel after it had been conquered by the Babylonians. He was assassinated by Jewish zealots — disgruntled Jewish monarchists — and after his death, the Jews were cleaned out of the land of Israel and shipped off to a Babylonian exile. So the Fast of Gedalyah marks the beginning of the Jewish Diaspora — the exile.

This series of fasts tells our bodies and our souls the story of the encroachment of emptiness, the story of impermanence. There was a Great Temple, a great nation with its capital in Jerusalem, but even such seemingly unshakable institutions as these simply slipped away into the mists of history. But as we mentioned earlier, even while it stood, the Great Temple was a structure centered around emptiness. The Holy of Holies, the Sacred Center that all the elaborate structural elegance of the Temple only served to focus on, was primarily a vacated space. It was defined that way. The Holy of Holies was the space no one could enter except the high priest, and even he could only enter for a few moments on Yom Kippur. If anyone else entered this place, or if the high priest entered on any other day, the charged emptiness at the Sacred Center, the powerful nothingness there, would overwhelm him and he would die.

On Tisha B'Av, it is as if this emptiness breaks loose from its bounds and swallows everything up. The Temple burns. The emptiness once confined to the center of the Temple now characterizes it completely. The Temple is an emptiness.

This image touches us deeply. We are always under siege. And it is precisely the emptiness at the center of our lives that holds us under siege. Terrified of this emptiness, seeing it as utter negation, we defend against it with all our might. We struggle mightily to construct an identity, but the walls keep falling down, and then the city finally collapses, and the identity we have been laboring so desperately to shore up collapses along with it.

Several years ago, my wife and I wrote a book together, a spiritual autobiography entitled *One God Clapping: The Spiritual Path of a Zen Rabbi*. Sherril and I struggled as hard as we could to tell the absolute truth of my life, and in fact the book won some awards and reviewers praised it for its honesty. But after the book was published, I became painfully aware that of course we didn't get it absolutely right. How could we have? Who really understands what their life is about? And even to the extent that we did get it right, the emphasis is on the word "did," because identity constantly changes, and the meaning of our lives changes as well. What was true when we started working on the book was no longer completely true two years later, when the book came out, because life never stands still. Nothing does, not even our understanding of things that happened long ago. In any case, as luck would have it, the book was rather popular, and so I ended up flying all over the country promoting a kind of cartoon identity I no longer believed in with very much conviction. It was uncomfortable to do this, it made me feel like a bit of a fraud, but what was interesting was that I found this fraudulent feeling to be quite familiar. I realized that the discomfort I felt on this book tour was only a slight exaggeration of what was always going on with me and I suspect with you as well. We spend a great deal of time and energy propping up our identity, an identity we realize at bottom is really a construct. So it is that we are always living at some distance from ourselves.

My experience on the book tour was a kind of mild and relatively harmless version of an insight that often comes to us at much greater cost. Sometimes it takes a deep depression or even an emotional breakdown to communicate to us that we are living at too great a distance from the truth, that we are holding on to a myth about ourself that no longer applies. In my office I often see congregants who just can't let go of their idea of what they want their children to be — what they think they should be — until their kids have to break out of these ideas, often violently or traumatically. And husbands and wives hold on so hard to their idea of what their spouse used to be that they fail to notice that he or she has changed and is no longer that way at all. Nor are we very quick to notice that we ourself have changed and that the old ideas we have about ourself no longer conform to reality. We live in a state of siege, trying to prop up an identity that keeps crumbling, and that we secretly intuit to be empty. Then Tisha B'Av comes, and the walls begin to crumble, and then the entire city collapses, but something persists — something fundamentally nameless and empty, something that endures when all the walls have fallen down.

Intimations of the Ain Sof, the infinitely powerful nothingness at both the outer edges and the center of our universe, crowd out everything we would believe or know or feel. Or in the words of Meursault, the tormented antihero of Albert Camus' *The Stranger:*

> Nothing, nothing had the least importance, and I knew quite well why. He, too, knew why. From the dark horizon of my future a sort of slow, persistent breeze had been blowing toward me, all my life long, from the years that were to come. And on its way that breeze had leveled out all the ideas that people tried to foist on me in the equally unreal years I then was living through.

We are limited and finite, and every perception we form, every idea we have, is doomed to be pulled down by the weight of its own limitation. Everything we want or aspire to seems empty when we attain it. Everything we are seems empty. As soon as we say "I am this way" or "she is like that," we are immediately struck with the realization that it isn't true or that the opposite is true as well. Deep down we know; what we see of the world is not really the way the world is but merely the way we are capable of perceiving it, the product of the limited capacities of our eyes, our ears, our minds, and our hearts. Deep down we know; however the world was one moment ago, it no longer is. It has changed.

Those of us who meditate have a particularly intimate familiarity with the impossibility of stopping points. When we meditate we strive for silence, stillness, balance, and focus, yet the more we attain these things, the more we see that they are all impossible. If we meditate in the city, we might be troubled by occasional voices crying out and the *whoosh, whoosh, whoosh* of the cars going by on the streets. But if we were to meditate in a rural environment we would realize that the city is really a rather quiet place compared to the aural cacophony of crickets, birds, animal cries, and wind and water noises the country presents us with. Yet even if we were absolutely cut off from all noise, thrust into a sensory deprivation tank with no aural stimulus whatsoever, the din of our breathing and even the sound of our heart beating and our blood rushing through our veins would be overwhelmingly loud.

Nor is stillness a possibility either. The stiller we are, the more we see this to be true. No one can be absolutely still. When we are relatively still, we feel the constant motion that's going on in our bodies most acutely. We feel the subtle shifting for balance, the constant collapse of the muscles that hold us erect, the constant need to shore them up.

And the more focused our awareness, the more we realize how impossible it is to sustain that focus for any appreciable amount of time. The mind continually produces thoughts, and those thoughts inevitably carry our awareness away. And we are not even aware that this is going on until we manage to become fairly conscious of our mental functioning — fairly focused. Only then do we become aware of the impossibility of continuous mindfulness.

Finally, the more we focus on ourselves, the more we realize that we are not merely ourselves. Sitting in a room with others, consciously breathing the same air, hearing the same sounds, feeling our thoughts and our emotions moving in the same rhythmic patterns, we come to experience that we ourselves are not fixed objects, neither discrete nor separate, but part of a web of being larger than ourselves.

There are no stopping points, no hard, fixed places. Everything is in flux. Something in us needs to define and to aspire and to construct an identity. Form may well be emptiness, but as the Buddhists remind us in the very next breath, emptiness is also form. Form is necessary and inevitable to our experience, either part of our equipment as human beings or part of the endowment of the universe. We can't live without constructing forms, but something in us also understands the futility of the enterprise. Something in us never completely loses touch with the wind of the Ain Sof. We can't help erecting houses, and the houses will inevitably fall down. As long as we struggle to keep the houses erect, we will suffer.

3. A Place of Emptiness and Flow

Rabbi Gedalyah Fleer, a contemporary interpreter of the teachings of Rebbe Nachman, sees the emptiness at the center of the Temple sanctuary as the feature that made the sanctuary both a sacred and a healing space. Fleer cites a famous midrash about the Great Temple and its magical capacity to hold all of Israel at certain times of the year, in spite of the fact that its dimensions were far too small for such a huge number of people to occupy it all at once. The sanctuary, according to Fleer, was a malleable, protean space that could hold more than it looked like it could hold and was not diminished by the things it contained. In other words, it was a fluid space, a light, life-giving, flexible, flowing space, and this is what made it sacred and gave it the capacity to heal. Suffering, according to Rebbe Nachman, is an inflexibility. It arises when the flow of our lives has been stopped up.

Suffering is the result of an inappropriate holding on, a clinging, an excessive belief in the substance and the permanence of the things of this world. We cling to the familiar. The mime Marcel Marceau once said that the key to the illusions he created was simply to trick us into completing the archetypal pictures we all have in our minds. We are constantly doing this anyway, constantly imposing our primal trauma on the reality of the moment, and shaping reality so that it conforms to the archetypal picture we have of the world. Never mind that this is often a disappointing picture — even a heartbreaking picture. The disappointment we know somehow seems less frightening than the unknown heartbreak that might await us. Our expectations freeze the world in its tracks and force it to come out the way we expect it will. When we let go of this picture, the real world begins to flow again. We may be quite comfortable with the guilt that has been lodged in our psyche all our life. After all it is *our* guilt. Never mind that it has paralyzed us; we are familiar with it. In fact we may be so comfortable with it that we have failed to notice we have married a woman who can produce it in us exactly the same way our mother did. Until we are ready to let go of this guilt, we will continue to confuse our wife with our mother, to live and relive an outworn pattern instead of allowing our life to proceed with its natural flow. We will continually distort and clog up our life to fit the primal picture we are clinging to so tenaciously.

We cling to pain as well. Sometimes we do this to protect ourselves against the next time we might encounter a similar situation and be hurt again, like a person who believes that if she holds on to her fear of the plane crashing and never lets it go, the plane won't crash.

Or we cling to pain as a form of validation. The more we focus on our pain, the more we can see ourselves as a victim and the perpetrator of our pain as a villain, the more we feel free to ignore any responsibility we might have for our pain.

Or we cling to pain because we believe it to be an essential part of our being. We have suffered so deeply and for so long that we come to believe that we are our suffering and that our suffering is us. But clearly it is not, and the proof of this is that beyond our pain there is an essential part of our being that knows we are in pain. Thich Nhat Hanh, the great Vietnamese meditation teacher, often has his students visualize that they are like a tree bending in the winds of a gale on the top of a mountain. "If we look up, we shall see our branches bending as if they are about to break and be carried away by the storm. But if we look down, we shall know that the roots of the tree are held firmly in the earth, and we shall feel more stable and at rest." This is what we are like, Thich Nhat Hanh insists, when we feel overcome by vehement emotions, when we feel we are about to be swept away by despair, anxiety, anger, or fear. At such times we come to believe that we are our emotions; but we are not. Emotions come and go, but we are always here. We identify with the bending tree, when we could just as easily identify with the mountain, solid and unbent by the storm, and rooted firmly in the universe.

We also cling to pleasure. We hold on to it as tightly as we can because we don't quite believe it is real, while at the same time we are terrified of losing it. Sharon Salzberg writes that whatever happiness we experience carries with it a strong undercurrent of fear. When things are going well, when we are experiencing pleasure, when we are getting what we want, we feel obliged to defend our happiness because it seems so fragile, so unstable. Because our happiness feels as if it is in constant need of protection, we deny the very possibility of suffering. We cut ourselves off from facing it in ourselves and in others because we are afraid it will undermine or destroy whatever good fortune life has brought us, and because, once again, we feel the intimation of the Ain Sof deep down. Deep down we know this pleasure to be not only impermanent but empty as well.

So according to Rabbi Fleer, to locate sacred space — to locate healing — a leave-taking is necessary, a letting go. We must let go of the familiar, of our pain and our pleasure, and give the potential of the present moment a chance to flow through us. This is why sacred space is vacated space, a place of emptiness and flow.

Shabbat is a sacred space, a time full of no-thing, no activity, no creative work. A time when according to the Torah we must *shavat vayinafash* — stop and re-ensoul ourselves, stop and breathe again, stop and allow ourselves to fill up with the great wind of the Ain Sof once more.

Meditation is a sacred space as well. In meditation we leave our ordinary unconscious state and enter a state of mindfulness, a state where we simply breathe in, let go of the breath, and breathe in again; a state where we watch the mind continuously producing forms, and where we continually let go of these forms and return our awareness to the breath; a state where we become conscious again of the Ain Sof, the nothingness that heals us from the suffering which inevitably arises out of our clinging to form. In meditation we inhabit each moment without holding on to it or wishing it were some other part of the flow, some other arc on the endless circle of being. In meditation we see ourselves not as a fixed object nor as a discrete self, but as a part of an interdependent whole.

We see ourselves as the Psalmist sees us:

Adonai, you have been our refuge through all generations.
Before mountains emerged, before the earth was formed,
From age to age, everlastingly, you are God.
But humans you crumble into dust, and say "Return,
    mortals!"
For a thousand years in your sight are as a passing day,
    a watch in the night.
You engulf all human beings in sleep.
They flourish for a day like grass.
In the morning it sprouts afresh;
By nightfall it fades and withers. . . .
We may live seventy years,

Or if we are very strong, eighty years,
All laden with trouble and travail. . . .
Who can know the strength of your anger or the awe
    we should feel in your presence?
Teach us to be mindful of our days, so that a heart of
    wisdom may come to us. . . .

— Psalm 90

When we meditate, we see ourselves as waves on an endless sea. Each wave on the sea is essentially empty of its own being, rising up and then falling away again, but the sea itself endures.

We see ourselves as the naturalist Richard Nelson sees himself in *The Island Within*, his wonderful memoir of life on the Inside Passage of southeastern Alaska, a region I know and love very well myself. Nelson writes of watching the end of the salmon's cycle of life, death on a massive scale — dead and dying fish drifting past him in huge numbers as he stands along the shore. At first he finds himself lapsing into tragic memories, depressed by so much naked death. But as he watches, he begins to realize that something besides simple death is taking place. The dead fish are decaying, dissolving in the current, and then filtering into the rock and the sand and becoming part of the stream, the island, the ocean, and the earth itself. Hatchling fish will feed on nutrients left by all this death.

A new generation of fish will ripen from the bodies of the old, flow out into the sea, grow there by feeding on other life and then return. Like all else that lives, the salmon are only bits of earth, shaped for a moment into fish, then taken back again, to emerge as other life. This same transformation has repeated itself in Bear Creek each fall for thousands of years, and on the island since it rose up at the continent's edge, and on earth since the first organisms scuttled in the depths of the Paleozoic sea. . . . The salmon are not independent organisms but tiny parts of one great organism that contains them all, the living flesh that grows from earth and covers its surfaces. . . . How can there be a final, absolute death if life as a whole, or earth itself, is the organism? What I've dreaded about death is the prospect of leaving, of lapsing into a nothingness beyond life. But in this endless process of metamorphosis, there can be no final death, only a transmutation of life. A flowing through. A constantly changing participation in the living community. And the fate of all living things is an earthbound immortality.

Life is a powerful emptiness that expresses itself in myriad forms all joined in the no-thing from which they arose and which goes on beyond them, beyond us. When we let go of these forms, the whole of life begins to flow through us, and we feel the profound comfort of knowing we can never be separate from anything. We are part of an undifferentiated oneness made entirely of movement, a chorus full of disembodied voices. That woman in the pink satin nightgown who was dying in Colma was right; everything is indeed music. If we let go of our pain and our fear, we can dance to this music, our arms and our legs and our torso moving fluently to it, giving witness, giving form to its fervent, invisible pulse.

PRACTICE POINTS

Following the Breath as It Arises out of Nothing and Falls Away into Nothing Again

In this practice and the ones that follow in this chapter, we will repeat some of the material we covered at the end of the first chapter, but with a particular emphasis on pointing us toward the kind of emptiness we have been discussing here. Focusing on the breath is particularly useful in this regard.

The breath is life. Sitting in meditation, eyes half closed, awareness focused on the breath, this is perfectly clear. The breath is life, and the breath comes out of nowhere and returns to nothing again. Breathing out, we experience a small moment of faith. Perfectly attuned to this moment, we realize that we are releasing the breath into a void. We don't know where it is going and we don't know where it comes from. Yet the next moment, there it is again, out of nothing; literally out of nowhere, the breath has returned. The breath is life, and life comes out of nowhere, fills our body, animates it, and then returns to nowhere again. We experience this every time we breathe in and breathe out again. The breath, which itself is only emptiness moving, comes out of emptiness and returns to it.

The Body as Tabernacle: The Sacred Emptiness at the Center

The body has its own sacred architecture. When we sit for meditation on the floor, our legs are crossed or folded under us symmetrically. Or in a chair, they are symmetrically folded at the knees in front of us, the balls of our feet finding balance for us. As we tilt our hips forward, we feel a lift running up the central column of our torso, an energy pushing up at the sternum and the crown of the skull. This energy illuminates the body's perfect symmetry, the symmetry of matter on either side of this lifting energy: our two arms, held at our sides at the balance point between tension and relaxation; our two hands, held at this same balance point; the banks of pectoral muscles on either side of our chest; our two breasts, our eyes, our ears. The body is perfectly balanced, a perfectly doubled structure pointing in to the center. As we sit in meditation with our eyes half closed, all this symmetry and the inrush of breath create a strong inward momentum. As our awareness follows the breath, we find ourselves being pulled into the sacred center, a place of light and air, of thoughts and impulses, in short, a place of no-thing. The matter, the stuff of our body, is also a perfectly harmonious shape, which, like all such forms, points toward its center, a place devoid of matter and stuff. So it is that we come to experience the emptiness at the center of our lives, the formlessness at the center of form.

Stillness, Silence, Balance, Focus:
The Impossibility of Stopping Points

Sitting still, aware of our stillness, we are aware that we are never really still. The stiller we are, the clearer our focused awareness, the clearer this is. We are always moving. There is no stopping point. The back will not remain erect but is in constant need of shoring up. The hips give way, and that wonderful forward thrust we managed to attain, which sent all the weight and tension in our body falling down to the legs, and sent that lift up through the torso, collapses without our noticing and we have to thrust the hips forward again. The chin falls to the hollow of the collarbone. The back stiffens. The eyelids flutter. Sitting very still and wide awake, we are aware of what a shifting, gelatinous mass we are, constantly moving, stretching and collapsing, never completely still, yet relatively still — still enough to notice we are not completely still.

And we are silent. Except of course for the rushing of the breath, or the whoosh of the traffic outside, or a distant conversation. We have to be relatively silent, to see how much noise there is in our silence, how impossible true silence really is. As impossible as sustained focus, for example. We resolve to anchor our awareness in our breathing and our body, and we do, to a certain extent, but the more we succeed in focusing our awareness on these things, the more we discover how impossible it is to sustain. The mind continuously produces thoughts, and eventually these thoughts carry our awareness away.

So it is that we experience that the world is in flux, that there are no stopping points. So it is that we experience the truth. Still, silent, balanced, and focused, we experience the impossibility of these states. Yet without being still, silent, balanced, and focused, we cannot enter this flow. Moving around, making noise, unbalanced, and unfocused, we come to believe in a false world, a static world full of fixed objects, fixed states with beginnings, middles, and ends.

Thich Nhat Hanh: Tree on a Mountain in a Storm

Thich Nhat Hanh suggests the following meditation. Visualize yourself as a tree on the top of a mountain during a terrible storm. The wind and rain are blowing through your branches so fiercely that you are genuinely afraid you will be uprooted. He writes, "When we are oppressed by emotions, we feel very insecure and fragile, we may even feel that we are in danger of losing life itself."

We begin by identifying with the tree to attune ourselves to this psychological reality.

But why continue to identify with the tree? Why not identify instead with the mountain, as solid and immovable as the universe and unthreatened by any storm? After all, our roots go down into the mountain, and really we are quite stable. If we are the tree, we are also the mountain. There is no need for us to identify only with the most vulnerable, unstable part of what we are.

If we know how to withdraw from the storm, we will not be swept away. We must transfer our attention to a place about two fingers' width below the navel and breathe deeply. We recite a silent formula in harmony with our breathing. Breathing in, we say, "Breathing in, I see myself as a mountain." Breathing out, we say, "Breathing out, I feel solid." "In doing this," Thich Nhat Hanh concludes, "we shall see that we are not just our emotions. Emotions come and go, but we are always here."

Chapter Six

In the Transformed World

1. Unmasking the World

WE BEGAN THE LAST CHAPTER WITH A DISCUSSION OF
Hanukkah, one of two Talmudic holidays, the postbiblical holidays that didn't come into being until Israel was already living in
exile. As such, these two holidays reflect the two great polarities of
the long Jewish exile — assimilation and annihilation. Hanukkah
is the story of the heroic Jewish resistance to a Hellenist attempt
to wipe out Judaism. The Jews of the Hanukkah story were free to
live in peace if only they would consent to give up Jewish practice.
Led by the Maccabees, the Jews refused to give up their covenant
with God and prevailed in their rebellion against the Syrian Hel-
lenists. In the Purim story, the Jewish people were threatened with

annihilation regardless of their relationship to Jewish practice. This holiday celebrates their miraculous salvation from an early Persian manifestation of ethnic cleansing and genocide.

As resonant — as prescient — as these historical concerns may be, they tend to overshadow the very powerful spiritual suggestions of these holidays. Hanukkah, as we discussed earlier, is also the festival of light at the darkest moment of the year, the story of the great light that arose out of nothing at all. Purim is the story of the unmasking of God. Nothing is what it appears in the Purim story. Esther conceals her Jewishness from the Persians. The wicked Haman is the masked karmic reiteration of Amalek, grandson of Esau and Israel's timeless nemesis. Even God is disguised in the Purim story.

"When does the Torah mention the Purim story?" the rabbis of the Talmud ask. (Of course the Torah never really does mention the Purim story; the events described in the book of Esther take place thousands of years after the close of the Torah.) "In the book of Deuteronomy, when God says '*Astir panai*' — 'I will hide my face.'" This is a particularly ingenious answer. First of all, the word *astir* is spelled with the same consonants as Esther, the heroine of the Purim story (it is vocalized with different vowels, of course, but vowels aren't indicated in the Torah, so it looks like exactly the same word). The meaning of this phrase fits perfectly as well. God literally hides his face in the book of Esther. His name is never even mentioned in it — yet we can feel the presence of God very powerfully in the book's odd web of chance and significant coincidence.

The wicked Haman procures the king's favor with silver and has the king issue a decree ordering everyone to bow down to him.

Mordecai the Jew refuses to do so. Enraged, Haman conspires to have the king issue a decree calling for the annihilation of all the Jews in the kingdom. The king, of course, has no idea that his own wife, Queen Esther, is also a Jew. Esther just happened to be chosen from all the virgins in the kingdom to be his queen a short time before this. Mordecai, who is Esther's uncle, just happens to overhear two men plotting to assassinate the king and turns them in to the authorities. This deed just happens to be recorded in the official chronicles of the court, and when the king has a terrible case of insomnia and wants to read these chronicles to put himself to sleep, he just happens to turn to the passage that describes Mordecai's loyalty to him regarding the assassins. So it is that the king plucks Mordecai from Haman's evil clutches and elevates him to a position of honor in his court. This is the beginning of Haman's unraveling. When the king discovers that both Mordecai and his beloved Esther are Jews, he becomes enraged at Haman for involving him in his evil scheme. Nor does it hurt that when Haman goes to beg Esther for mercy, the king walks into her chamber just in time to see Haman hurl himself prostrate onto her lap as she reclines on her marriage couch. Happily for the Jews, the king misinterprets the scene. "Does he mean to ravish the queen in my own palace?" the king exclaims. When the decree of annihilation is still hanging over them, Mordecai orders all the Jews of the kingdom to pray and to fast, although the book of Esther does not stipulate to whom. This string of remarkable coincidences is clearly presented by the book of Esther as the answer to all this praying and fasting, the finger of an utterly invisible and unmentioned God manipulating all the action in the background.

On Purim we acknowledge that God is disguised in the world and that the world itself is God's costume. There is no particle, no corner of this world, that is empty of God's presence, yet this presence is rarely obvious nor even manifest at all. God is masked by the world, by its forms, by our emotional impulses, by nature, and by language, and this is not a modern phenomenon. God has appeared to be absent from the world in every age, and it has always been the burden of spiritual practice to unmask God and to bring his presence out of hiding again.

2. Through the Breath and Beyond the World of Form

How did God create the world? If the account at the beginning of the book of Genesis is correct, God spoke the world into being out of nothing. God said, Let there be light, and there was light. God said, Let there be an expanse in the midst of the water called sky, and let the earth sprout vegetation, and let there be lights in the expanse of the sky, and let the waters bring forth swarms of living creatures and birds that fly above the earth across the expanse of the sky, and so it was. And when God spoke these things, they all burst out of nothingness and into being.

There was only one exception to this rule: us. Human beings were not merely spoken into being. We were created by a different method. We were breathed into life. "The Lord God formed man from the dust of the earth. God blew into his nostrils the breath [spirit] of life and man became a living soul."

According to Rebbe Nachman, this difference points to a distinctive hallmark of human spiritual consciousness. We human beings are connected to God through the breath. That is to say, it is the breath that connects us to that part of our experience which is deeper than form, deeper than language. Language is the implement of form. But the breath is both deeper and more primal than form. We can breathe without speaking, but we can't speak without breathing. The breath comes first. The breath goes deeper. The breath connects us to the thing itself and not just the word for the thing. The breath connects us to the present-tense reality of the world and not some formal representation of that moment. God lives in that moment too, so to enter that moment through the breath is to enter into an encounter with God, to unmask God, to penetrate the forms of the world that are God's disguise.

This is what the Zohar, the seminal medieval compendium of Jewish mysticism, means when it says that God breathed of himself into Adam. We are created in the image of God, which is to say, we live by virtue of the spirit/breath of God. The breath, according to Rebbe Nachman, is identical to the *chiyah* — the life force — the defining spiritual quality that makes us uniquely what we are and sustains us in life. This is why the rabbis always equated life with the capacity to breathe. If the breath stops, life is considered to have ended (a holding that still prevails in Orthodox Jewish law, and that has caused some tension for Orthodoxy as medical communities increasingly recognize the cessation of brain activity as the official mark of death).

Adam and Eve, the Zohar continues, were created last so that they could bring creation back to its source in God. All creatures breathe, but only humans breathe consciously. Human consciousness, through its capacity to see beyond forms and language and to recognize in the breath the primal level of being, connects creation with its creator.

This, according to the Zohar, is the solution to a famous problem that bewildered the rabbis for a long time. As we have mentioned, the Torah says of Shabbat that on that day, God *shavat vayinafash* — God stopped creating and was re-ensouled, re-inspirited, refreshed again. The problem is that as our model for the observation of Shabbat, God should have stopped creating *before* Shabbat and not on the day of Shabbat itself. Rashi and many of the other commentators raise this problem, but they never really solve it. It just *seemed* as if God was stopping on Shabbat, they say, but really it's just that God has a much more precise sense of time than we have, and his stopping was so close to Shabbat that it seemed to spill over onto Shabbat itself, although that was just an illusion.

Not a very satisfactory solution, to be sure. But if we read *shavat vayinafash* as "stopped [speaking] and breathed again," the problem disappears. Shabbat observance is no longer an issue, and the meaning of this verse becomes that for six days God spoke the world into being, and on the seventh day, God stopped speaking and went back to breathing again, and all the forms that had come into being by virtue of God's speaking were now perpetuated in their beingness by the natural flow of God's breath.

The rabbis of the Kabala had a rather literal belief in the notion that language masked a deeper sense of reality. Moshe Cordovero of Safed, the great sixteenth-century Kabalist, said that every letter of the Hebrew alphabet contains "worlds and souls and Godhead. [The letters are] like bodies or palaces for the spiritual forces from above which they contain, like the body into which the soul was infused." When we pronounce these letters out loud — when we join them to the breath — these elements and forces emerge from the letters and become manifest; once again we are in touch with that deeper and more primal sense of experience that language and form can only point to.

As we mentioned earlier, Rebbe Nachman defined suffering as being afraid of things we don't need to be afraid of; in this he too was talking about form. Gedalyah Fleer fleshes out this idea as follows. We imagine that something presents a threat to us, or that we can't control it, or that it might impinge on our being. This thought may very well have a more visceral root, but by the time it reaches our awareness, it is a formal construct, a melodrama made of language. We lose sight of the breath. We develop an excessive — an absolute — belief in the reality of a particular form — an idea, a construct — and this belief blocks the possibility of fluidity, the ongoingness of the breath. That's why when we fall into a panic, people instinctively tell us, "Just take a deep breath." Breathing is more primal, more real than form. Back in touch with what is common to all things — the soul of all things, the life force, the breath — we are no longer frightened by the phantoms of the world of form. Breath calms us down, relieves pain, and expands our awareness, creating space for us, relieving us from the contracted and limited world of language and concept.

When I was a Zen student, I had a friend who came from a long line of doctors. Like me, he had come to California after college to study Zen, but after many years as a Zen student, he realized that there was no escaping the family karma: he had to become a doctor, as every male in his family had done as far back as anyone could remember. At first, though, he had a terrible time in medical school. He couldn't focus on the lectures; it was all a lot of talk to him, and he failed the first round of exams quite miserably. So the Zen master suggested that he try another tack altogether. "Don't even try to listen to the lectures. Don't take notes, and don't try to follow what your teachers are saying," the Zen master said. "Just breathe with them. When they breathe in, you breathe in. When they breathe out, you breathe out." My friend was skeptical, but he had very little to lose. He was very close to flunking out. So he tried it. It worked. He soon found himself resonating with his teachers very deeply, understanding them implicitly. Working from this ground of profound empathy, it became an easy step to understand their ideas. He did very well in medical school after that and is now a fine doctor.

Sound is the near cousin of breath. Sound is made out of breath. Like breath, sound is more primary than language, sound is preformal. As children, we are born to a world of breath and pure sound. At first everyone responds to our breathing, and then to the noises we make, but as time goes on, and little by little, these sounds acquire form and become words and concepts. No one pays attention to the sounds we make anymore. We become so infatuated with, so attached to language, concept, and form that we forget all about the world of breath, sound, and gesture they emerged from.

The psychologist Jean Piaget formed his brilliant theories of child development not by studying books or attending classes, but rather by getting down on the floor with small children and observing their development firsthand. He noticed that before children learned to speak, they communicated through a series of sounds and gestures. When they wanted to communicate "no," they might do so with a grunt and an emphatic wave of the hand. As they learned to speak, the grunt and the wave gradually gave way to speech, to the word "no." Every time the child said "no," both the sound and the gesture diminished, but neither one of them ever completely fell away. Even as an adult, the child retained an imperceptible vestige of them, an inaudible grunt, an inchoate wave. That's why speech is so visceral, so powerful, so galvanized by the force of gesture. There is always something of the gesture in speech, always something of sound, and these things keep us connected to the primal world even as we speak.

Yet there is a reality even deeper than sound and gesture, an emptiness beyond these forms. Before we go too far with this idea that language is a less profound medium than silence and breathing, it must be acknowledged that our seminal revelation, the giving of the Torah on Mount Sinai, was both verbal and extremely noisy, filled with both language and sound. In the account of this event in the book of Exodus, we read that the Torah was given amidst "thunder and lightning . . . and the voice of a horn that was exceedingly loud, and when the people heard it, they trembled and stood afar off." The Torah itself is inescapably verbal — literally made out of language. Yet the rabbis of the Talmud heard something beneath all this verbiage and cosmic din, as the following midrash from Shir ha-Shirim Rabbah attests:

> Rabbi Abahu said in the name of Rabbi Yochanan: When the Holy One gave the Torah, no bird called out, no flying creature flapped its wings, no oxen lowed, no *ofanim* [a kind of angel] flew and no *serafim* [another kind of angel] said "Holy, Holy, Holy," the sea didn't wave, and human beings didn't speak. Rather, the entire world was silent and still and a voice went out, "I am the Lord your God."

How could the rabbis contradict the account of the Torah so thoroughly? How could they say that the Torah emerged from a profound and utter silence, when the Torah itself describes something entirely different, a terrifying and unbearable din? In my Buddhist days I once attended a ritual called the Black Hat Ceremony performed by the Karmapa Lama, a very high figure in the Tibetan Buddhist religious hierarchy. The Karmapa went all around the country performing this ritual, and the ceremony became a kind of gathering of the clan for the various American Buddhist communities. San Francisco had the largest such community at the time, and we all gathered there in a huge warehouse at the end of a long pier at San Francisco's Fort Mason. Thousands of people from all the various Buddhist traditions — Tibetan Buddhists, Zen Buddhists, and so forth — came with meditation cushions and blankets. Many brought their families, and there was a disappointingly picniclike atmosphere; everyone was talking at once, and the screams of the hundreds of young children were bouncing off the blank warehouse walls. The din was unbearable, and the wait was very long — the Karmapa was several hours late.

The idea of the Black Hat Ceremony was that when the Karmapa put on a certain black hat, he became Avalokiteshvara, the Bodhisattva of compassion. When the Karmapa and his monks finally appeared, the ceremony got under way very quickly. The Karmapa sat on a platform in preternatural stillness — he looked inhuman, like a painted Buddha — while the monks began to blow on long, crude horns that made a sound like a thousand elephants trumpeting. Everyone stopped talking, but the children screamed even louder, and now the noise was truly insupportable. But when other monks took the big, black, three-cornered hat out of an elaborate hatbox and placed it on the Karmapa's head, the din was replaced by a dazzling silence. One could still see the open mouths of the children who had been screaming a moment before, and the monks still had their lips pressed against the mouthpieces of the horns and their cheeks were still puffed up with breath, but no sound issued forth, neither from the children nor from the horns. The room was suffused with a white sheet of silent light. Years later, when I read the midrash about the silence at Mount Sinai, I realized that that was what I had experienced in that warehouse at Fort Mason — the dazzling silence within sound itself, the profound emptiness out of which that form emerges. Sometimes when I am changing stations on a radio tuner, I realize that the sounds that come into the room from each station I tune to are just aspects — tiny slices — of the silence that was in the room before I turned the radio on, a silence that contains all sound, a silence from which all sound emerges. This is the silence of the breath. It is both deeper and more primal than any sound.

When we focus on the breath, when we anchor our awareness in it, we return to this primal world. We deepen our awareness quite literally. The belly is the locus of our breathing and the most important center of consciousness in our body, because it is here that we become aware of the primal world, of that aspect of our experience that is deeper than form. When we breathe in deeply, allowing the breath to come all the way down to the pit of the belly as it always wants to do anyway, we drink in the world very deeply as well. We bring it all the way down to this center of primary consciousness. When we breathe in a shallow way, engaging only the chest, we take in the world in a shallow way, leaving it up to the brain, a decidedly secondary sensory organ, to make sense of the world. The brain is bound by language and form. It cannot see beyond these things, and so it is that we become habituated to a thin world of ideas and concepts, a surface world of language and form.

Sitting in meditation, following the breath all the way to the pit of the belly, we follow the breath into a dimension of depth as well. As our awareness settles in the breath, the breath becomes more vibrant; it becomes radiant. Soon the mind becomes vibrant and radiant too, and this sense spreads until it has filled whatever world we occupy, whatever environment we inhabit.

On Shabbat we do no creative work, no creation of forms, no writing, no cooking, no building, no drawing — not even any ice skating, for fear of the forms our blades might leave in the ice. Instead we rest and get back to the breath. *Shavat vayinafash.* We stop and breathe again, and in doing so we emulate God and reconnect with him. We unmask God. We renew our connection to God by putting aside the implements of form and just being.

God is being. That, in fact, is God's name. When we breathe, we are. We bring God out of hiding. We are with God, silent and empty in the ongoing beingness of the breath.

•

Another framework for thinking about this business of unmasking God is the classical Kabalistic doctrine of the Four Worlds. According to the Kabala, there are four realms between the material world and the Ain Sof, God's essential being, the endless, infinitely powerful, and unknowable emptiness that surrounds all existence. The realm in which we are embodied — the realm of physicality and materiality — is called *asiyah,* the realm of action. This is where all impulses become manifest in the world. This is the world of the body and the hard object. This is the world in which molecules move so quickly we forget they are molecules and mistake them for things.

The next realm up is *yetzirah,* the realm of formation. This is an intermediate realm between conception and materiality, where the objects of the pure intellect begin to take form, to move from a kind of Platonic state, to *asiyah* and embodiment. It is the realm connected to language and to emotion. Language serves a similar intermediary function. It brings things out of the purely metaphysical realm and into the physical. This happens every time we speak. We have a metaphysical idea that we translate into language and then into speech, which has a physicality — which exists as sound waves in the world of *asiyah.* When someone hears us speak, the process is reversed. Sound waves enter the listener's body and are translated back into the metaphysical realm. Emotions also stand somewhere between the physical and metaphysical realms. Emotions are not physical events, yet unlike pure thought, they reverberate in the material realm. They cause our hearts to beat faster, tears to run down our cheeks, or our faces to turn red.

Briyah, or the realm of pure conception, is next. This is the realm of the intellect, an impulse expressing itself in the mind as pure idea.

Atzilut is the realm of pure spiritual emanation, which stands in closest proximity to the Ain Sof itself. This is a realm of pure, primal energy, formless waves of soul that will blossom as ideas in the world of *briyah.*

Each of these realms, it must be said, is an expression — an embodiment — of all the others. In the Ain Sof, the powerful emptiness which surrounds all this, nothing ever happens, nothing exists except as an infinitely charged potential. But when the Ain Sof expresses its will, this will emerges as a wave, a pure emanation in the world of *atzilut,* and when this wave penetrates mind in *briyah,* it becomes a conception, a pure, Platonic entity. From there it moves through the world of formation, *yetzirah,* acquiring form through language and feeling, until finally, in the world of *asiyah,* it acquires substance. It exists. It happens. So it is that the material world is God made manifest, God in the guise of materiality.

This is all from God's point of view. Where our own spiritual practice is concerned, things proceed the other way around. We begin at *asiyah* and work our way out to the Ain Sof. We begin at the body (*asiyah*) and work our way out through the heart (*yetzirah*) and the mind (*briyah*) and the spirit (*atzilut*) to the vast emptiness out of which the body emerged.

This is not a uniquely Jewish schema. We find this grid in many of the world's religions and spiritual practices. We find it, for example, in Buddhism, or at least, a very precise replication of it. In the Anapanasati Sutta, the Sutra on the Four Foundations of Mindfulness, we see the same movement from concentration on the breath and the body, to mindfulness of feelings, to an awareness of the mind itself, and then to concentration on the pure states beyond mind such as impermanence and cessation, and then finally on Shunyata, the great emptiness beyond all form. The first four foundations — body, feelings, mind, and the pure states beyond mind — are masks for this emptiness. We unmask them by practicing mindfulness.

We shouldn't be too compulsive or hierarchical about all this. If we should happen to arrive at the mind before the heart, or the soul before the mind, so be it. The main point, I think, is to begin in the breath and the body. This is where all spiritual practice worth its salt begins. This is the most accessible, the most dependable realm. The breath and the body are always available to us, always there, always a platform from which to begin our practice. We inhabit our breath and our body with consciousness, until this mindfulness flows over, to the heart, to the mind, to the soul, each stage unmasking itself as something deeper than we thought it was, until they've all given way to the Ain Sof, the unlimited, undifferentiated essential being of God, which lies behind every mask, beyond language, beyond nature, beyond desire, beyond the breath and the body itself.

3. Beyond the Veil of Nature

The Ba'al Shem Tov, the founder of Hasidic Judaism, has a wonderful commentary on the penultimate verse of the Eighty-fourth Psalm. "A sun and a shield is the Lord God [Lord=*Yud-heh-vuv-heh;* God=*Elohim*]." *Yud-heh-vuv-heh* (YHVH), the explicit and unpronounceable name of God, the Ba'al Shem explains, is here compared to the sun. Just as a barrier protects us from the direct light of the sun, so the word *Elohim* protects us from the word *Yud-heh-vuv-heh.* This is why the words "sun" and "shield" are used in parallel relationship to the words "Lord" and "God." It is impossible to stare into the sun because of the power of the light that emanates from it. Because of the weakness of our vision, the Ba'al Shem continues, we couldn't benefit from the light of the sun at all if it weren't for a shield or a curtain that protects us from it. So it is with the name *Yud-heh-vuv-heh.* It is a very great light — too great for us by far. The power of the light that emanates from it needs to be reduced and limited by the name *Elohim*. What is *Elohim?* The name *Elohim* has the same *gematria* as the word *ha-tevah* (nature, literally, "the nature"). So nature is the shield through which it is possible for us to perceive the light of God.

I think this interpretation might need a little interpretation itself. What is *gematria?* In Hebrew the letters of the alphabet are also numbers, so every word has both a meaning and a numerical value, or *gematria*. In Jewish mysticism, when two words have the same numerical value, they are thought to correspond to each other in some way, to have the same spiritual quality; in effect, to be the same thing. The word *Elohim* consists of the letters *aleph* (1), *lamed* (30), *heh* (5), *yud* (10), and *mem* (40), for a total numerical value of 86. *Ha-tevah* (nature) consists of the letters *heh* (5), *tet* (9), *vet* (2), and *ayin* (70), and also has a total numerical value of 86. So the God-name *Elohim* corresponds to the word *ha-tevah:* nature is the screen through which we are capable of seeing the light of God. Without this screen it would be impossible for us to see God's unadulterated light. Our human capacities are far too limited for this.

The truth of this has rarely been so apparent as it is in our day. We do not live in a God-infatuated age, in a time when people often speak of seeing or feeling the presence of God in their daily lives. It seems to me that the Purim story, in which God is never overtly seen, is the most accessible of all the biblical stories to modern readers, who also relate to God largely in terms of God's absence. But there are exceptions to this rule, and one of them is nature. People who never speak or think of God will return from a week of backpacking at Yosemite feeling that they have seen the reflection of God in a sunset or a waterfall or a sky

full of stars, or that they have heard God's voice in the primal roaring of the Yosemite headwaters.

Even when we are at home in our own houses, we may see
the light of God through the operations of nature in our bodies
and our lives. Birth and death, the two defining natural events of
our lives, communicate the presence of God very strongly. More
than once it has occurred to me that the main impetus for the precipitous burgeoning of interest in spirituality among members of
my generation might be that we were the first generation of
fathers invited into the delivery room as a matter of course, and
the first generation of mothers in a long time who experienced the
process of birth without being drugged insensate.

I lived through that transition. My oldest child was born
under the old system. No one was present for his birth at all. I was
downstairs in the waiting room reading a magazine and my wife
was unconscious. I'm not even sure that the doctor was present, or
perhaps he was barely so. He was due for a golfing holiday, and so
had called all his most advanced pregnancies into the hospital,
drugged all the mothers, and induced slightly premature births for
everyone. I assume he presided over these births himself before
leaving for that holiday, but I can't be sure, since I wasn't there
myself.

My second child was born under the new system. It was a
difficult labor fraught with fearful complications. We had wanted
a home birth, but that hope had been frustrated, and then we
thought we would have the birth in a cozy labor room at the hospital with a minimum of invasive medical technology. But the
labor reached a dangerous point, and the doctors insisted on using
the main delivery room, a most unromantic repository of invasive

technology that seemed utterly devoid of feeling, particularly of spiritual feeling. Yet when that baby came, we all experienced the most powerful feelings imaginable, and that operating room became a cathedral, with a powerful radiance emanating from the spiral surgical lamps on the ceiling.

We feel the presence of God as we face death as well, whether our own death or the death of those we love. I often sit at tables with families who have lost someone, reviewing the life of the person who has just died in preparation for the funeral. There is often a point in this process when there before us, the sacred miracle, the sacred shape of a human life, begins to make itself manifest, and the presence of the Artisan who crafted that shape becomes manifest as well. When we are ill, when our body ceases to function the way it was designed to, we stop taking that design and function for granted. We feel a sense of awe, a sense of how deeply, how intricately the Great Designer has touched our daily lives.

Yet it must be said, I feel the force of the Ba'al Shem's words most keenly when I am out in nature: at dusk, when the world becomes less distinct and one can feel the trees giving up their life force; at dawn, when there are only a few stars in the sky and one can hear God calling out each of their names; in a redwood forest, where one can feel the dead organic matter, the mulch on the forest floor, being driven upward by divine intelligence, by seeds and infinity, rising up, reaching toward the sun again; at the ocean, when the gravity of the sea and its infinite inventiveness — the limitless patterning of the waves as they smash themselves into oblivion against the shore — fills us with awe. If one is willing to relax one's grip at such times and let one's consciousness blur a little bit, intimations of God-light creep in through the screen of nature.

The writing of the environmentalist John Muir is full of this kind of awareness. He writes, for example, of a long winter he spent up at the timber line in the High Sierra. He noticed a very strange pine forest there, a forest of tuberculata (knobcone) pine, with two extremely puzzling features. First, none of the trees ever let go of their pine cones. The cones sat stuck very high up on the trees and never seemed to fall off. There wasn't a single pine cone on the entire forest floor. Second, all the trees in this forest were exactly the same age — the same height, with the same number of rings in their trunks. If the trees never let go of their pine cones, how would they ever reproduce? And who ever heard of a forest where all the trees were the same age? It was just as absurd as a human civilization where everyone was the same age would be — and just as unlikely. So John Muir was contemplating all this one day from a ridge just across from this forest, when a big summer storm boiled up. Thunder and lightning filled the horizon. And suddenly a bolt of lightning struck one of the tuberculata pines; the pine caught fire, and pretty soon the whole forest was ablaze. John Muir shortly had the answer to his twofold mystery: as if by the signal of an unseen hand, every tree in the forest suddenly dropped its pine cones at exactly the same moment. This was how the tuberculata pine had learned to survive in the unforgiving environment of the timber line. It had learned to hold on to its pine cones until a fire came and burned it down. It cast its seeds onto ground that was now unshaded and cleared of competing vegetation, giving the next generation a head start over plants that might otherwise shade it or crowd it out. This was why every tree in the forest was the same age. Muir was thunderstruck. He sat on the ridge trembling with awe in the face of the divine intelligence he had just seen revealed in all this.

In *My First Summer in the Sierra* Muir wrote about a time when he had hiked several days into the mountains outside Yosemite Valley and spent weeks in deep contemplation there, until he reached a state of complete and perfect attunement with the environment. He felt part of it, breathing in the oxygen the trees gave off and giving his own breath back to them; he felt the rise and fall of the forest, of his breath, of the light on the hills, to be one and the same. Then, all of a sudden, he felt the presence of Professor John Butler, his favorite teacher at the University of Wisconsin at Madison some twenty years earlier. He hadn't seen him since. They hadn't even corresponded, but he knew it for a certainty: John Butler had just entered his beloved Yosemite Valley. Even though it was late in the day, he started hiking down to the valley. It was all downhill and he made it in one fell swoop, arriving quite disheveled in his mountain garb early the next morning. He marched straight to the Ahwahnee Lodge, went to the desk clerk, and asked if there was a Professor John Butler registered there. Why in fact a professor had arrived at the inn the previous day, the desk clerk said, and he might very well be named Butler. The clerk checked the register, and there among the last arrivals was Professor John Butler's familiar handwriting. Muir recognized it immediately, even after twenty years.

Butler and his party had already gone up to the valley, and Muir finally tracked him down near Vernal Falls. Butler had been hiking by himself, and now he was stuck on a sheer cliff wall. Muir helped him down, no doubt saving his life. Professor Butler didn't even recognize Muir at first, so much did he look the wild mountain man, but then, of course, they had a joyous reunion, full of the wonder of what had just happened: Muir had not only known

Butler was there by some supernatural means, but he had arrived just in the nick of time to save his life. The professor began to quote from William Shakespeare: "There are more things in heaven and earth, Horatio, than are dreamt of in your philosophy." But Muir himself had a different take on what had happened. Later he would write:

> It seems strange that visitors to Yosemite should be so little influenced by its novel grandeur, as if their eyes were bandaged and their ears stopped. Most of those I saw yesterday were looking down as if wholly unconscious of anything going on about them, while the sublime rocks were trembling with the tones of the mighty chanting congregation of waters gathered from all the mountains round about, making music that might draw angels out of heaven. Yet respectable-looking, even wise-looking people were fixing bits of worms on bent pieces of wire to catch trout. Sport, they called it. Should church goers try to pass the time fishing in baptismal fonts while dull sermons were being preached, the so-called sport might not be so bad; but to play in the Yosemite temple, seeking pleasure in the pain of fishes struggling for their lives, while God himself is preaching his sublimest water and stone sermons!
>
> Now I'm back at the camp fire and cannot help thinking about my recognition of my friend's presence in the valley, while he was four or five miles away, and while I had no means of knowing that he was not thousands of miles away. It seems supernatural, but only because it is not understood. . . . Anyhow, it seems silly to make much of it while

the natural and common is more truly marvelous and mysterious than the so-called supernatural.

*Indeed, most of the miracles we hear of are infinitely less
wonderful than the commonest of natural phenomena when
fairly seen.* [Emphasis added.]

As I mentioned earlier, during several recent summers I've
had the privilege of spending some weeks in the Tebenkof
Wilderness in southeast Alaska. The wilderness here is protected
very carefully; only twelve human beings are permitted at a time.
As a consequence, it's one of the few places I've ever been to where
you can really feel the unadulterated cadences of nature. By day
the waters are full of salmon at the end of their breeding cycle,
making their joyful leaps out of the waters under the wistful eyes
of the black bears who lope along the shore, pull the salmon out of
the water with their bare paws, and then devour them. Eagles soar
above it all, swooping down from their bare treetop nests and then
returning to them. Whales run these waters too. The first sign of
them is the plume, a Leviathan breath made visible by sea spray.
Then you see the dark humped back arching just above the water.
This happens twice more, then the entire black mass turns a som-
ersault, leaving the flukes suspended in midair, a winged V atop a
column of black flesh. The flukes slap down hard against the surface of the sea. Then the whale dives, plunging deep, but if one
watches long enough, if one is very still, keeping an unwavering
eye on the water, the whale will breach again, full body upright,
extended, soaring high above the surface, all of this against an
endless array of colors and patterns in the air and on the surface of
the sea, an unimaginably variable palette of grays on cloudy days,

heartbreaking blues and greens when the sun is out and shining on the Tebenkof Mountains across the bay. At night, out on one of the islands, the moon rises bright yellow over the landfall, a shower of fiery meteors falls softly from the sky, the Northern Lights spread from horizon to horizon halfway up the sky, sending tendrils of light down to the rim of the earth. Wolves howl, loons hoot, salmon still leap out of the water and splash down again, and the whales can still be heard breathing deep in the sea while the stars whisper their endless secrets and the mountains sit listening quietly in long solemn rows, like jurors considering testimony of the utmost gravity. And this is testimony of the utmost gravity indeed. This sublime choreography, this heartbreaking dance of motion and light, this perfect harmony, gives witness to the infinite love of the choreographer. It is the perfect speech of God.

Although it requires a little more effort, we can hear this speech — feel this same choreography — in the urban natural environment as well. We can hear it in the rise and fall of city noises, human cries, and the susurration of the passing traffic. And we can feel it in this traffic very strongly if we let ourselves; if we stop saying "traffic" and just let the dance itself emerge. A car door opens, a car door closes, a kid runs out on the sidewalk, a woman comes out of the market and makes a beeline to the street at right angles to the kid. A car cuts quickly left onto a side street, while out on the boulevard the traffic seems to have a mind of its own as it moves in every direction at once. The boulevard *is* a mind. Big machines come and go, fueled by neither oil nor electricity but by consciousness; the stoplight suddenly turns green and releases a flow of cars in two directions. People on the sidewalk fall away into the periphery. At the gas station on the corner, a Chinese man fills up his tank; a blonde woman reads the meter and then puts the pump back in its place. Light attenuates. Dogs shuffle along according to their instincts. All of this reflects the infinite, multi-valent will of God, a will that emerges as a single and indivisible impulse out of an apparent chaos of volition.

How do we bring this will out of hiding, this music, this dance out from behind its veil? The secret is in the art of listening. When we meditate — when we follow the breath to a deeper and more primal place beyond form and language — we begin to accustom ourselves to that place. We begin to shift our focus to seeing the thing itself rather than giving so much attention to its name. We begin to listen and to see this way. When we hear the sound of cars passing by on the streets, we don't say "cars"; we just listen to the primary sound, the soft, breathy *whoosh* we hear outside. When birdsong invades our aural field, we don't say "bird"; instead we completely inhabit the primacy of that strange sound and its unearthly pulse. When we are out on the street in the traffic, we don't call it "traffic." We relax our grip on our awareness and allow it to become a little less distinct until we have a sense of the primary motion we are experiencing; until we are feeling the rhythm of it and not really seeing it at all.

So it is that *Elohim* and *ha-tevah* become one. So it is that while no one can peer directly into the face of God and live, we see God indirectly behind the veil of nature. So it is that we feel intimations of the reality that is deeper than language and meaning — that charged emptiness beyond the realm of form — in "the commonest of natural phenomena, fairly seen."

4. The Thing You Are Seeking Is Causing You to Seek

Rabbi Yitzchak of Akko, who lived in that Crusader port city in the Middle Ages, just before the great flowering of Safedian Kabala, told a wonderful story. Every ancient Jewish community depended on a man called a *batlan*. The *batlanim* were supported by the community (rather minimally to be sure) just to hang around until they were needed for some religious purpose such as completing a prayer minyan or attending a funeral.

One day, said Rabbi Yitzchak, one of these *batlanim* saw a beautiful princess coming out of the bathhouse. He sighed a deep sigh and said, "Would that I could do with her as I liked." "That will come to pass in the graveyard, but not here," the princess said. She meant to brush him off, of course, but he thought she was telling him to meet her at the graveyard for an assignation. So he went straight to the graveyard to wait for her, and there he devoted all his thoughts to her, thinking of her beauty. He waited there many days. After a while, because of his intense longing and his single-pointed concentration on this woman's form, his soul separated from all things sensual and material, including the woman herself, and he cleaved to God. Afterward, said Rabbi Yitzchak, this *batlan* became a perfect servant and holy man of God, and his blessings were beneficial to all who passed by.

The point of this story seems to be that even our basest impulses, sexual and otherwise, can mask a yearning for God, can point us toward the transcendent. The Talmud tells us that in the world to come, everyone will be called to account for the desires they might have fulfilled in this world but chose not to. The desires themselves are sacred. Who put them in our heart if not

God? But because we have been taught to be ashamed of what we want, our desires become horribly distorted and cause us to do hurtful things. Even a betrayal as painful as adultery might turn out to have its roots in a perfectly innocent impulse — in the desire to be loved, to have our experience be intense and exciting. If we could acknowledge these innocent desires, we might not feel compelled to act them out in such damaging ways.

The same is true of the desire for fame and success; we are conditioned to think that it is wrong to want these things, to be too ambitious. And the truth is we often do end up injuring both ourselves and others in pursuit of these desires. But underneath them may be the perfectly legitimate, even laudable need to use our God-given abilities to the utmost. The same God who gave us these abilities also gave us the desire to use them to their fullest capacity.

When we feel desire welling up inside us, we can usually imagine only two alternatives: to suppress the impulse or to act on it. But these are really two forms of the same idea — to get rid of the desire as best we can, to push it down or push it out. When we act on such feelings, we are often merely trying to exorcise them. We feel them in our heart and we feel threatened by them for one reason or another, so we try to get them out of our body and into the world by acting them out. This rarely if ever works. What really does seem to work with desire is to neither suppress it nor act on it, but rather to inhabit it, to honor it as the feeling God has given us at the moment, and to saturate this feeling with as much awareness as we can. This way we don't have to act out our desire in damaging ways. Having received the attention it needs, the desire will likely be content to fall away as quickly and mysteriously as it arose. With our consciousness firmly implanted in this impulse, it can more easily disclose its meaning to us. We are more likely to discover the legitimate need at the base of the desire or any other message it might have for us.

Our desires are neither base nor sinful in and of themselves. They are implanted in us by God to carry us along in our lives, to propel us down the path we need to follow. And if we could accept them as such, we probably wouldn't need to stab our best friend in the back or sleep with our wife's best friend.

In my autobiography, *One God Clapping*, I told the following story about my own secret desires and how they had shaped my life:

> When I was an infant, I got more attention than a Persian prince. My mother had three sisters, all living in the same building in Coney Island. I was my parents' first child, my aunts' first nephew, and my grandparents' first grandchild. I was the only baby in the family and everyone doted on me. But after a few years, all that changed. My aunts had children of their own, and then my father became quite ill and my sister had to undergo a series of operations on her leg. My mother now spent most of her time running back and forth between hospitals in Manhattan. In a few short years, I had gone from feast to famine, and as a consequence, I grew up with an insatiable thirst for attention.
>
> Now I often find myself in front of large groups of people, all focused on me and what I'm saying, and I've begun to realize that I have unconsciously manipulated my life to make this happen. I'm not completely comfortable with this; in fact, I'm quite uncomfortable with it and always have been. Back when all the attention was focused on my

father and sister, I knew that they really needed it and I didn't, so any desire for attention was clearly selfish, and when the desire welled up, as it always did, I felt horribly guilty. As I grew up, I hid out for many years, first in a cabin in faraway Mendocino County, then in a tiny room over a deli in Berkeley, and then in a monastery high in the Los Padres Mountains. Even when I first became a rabbi, I hid out in a small congregation, off in the woods, still trying to resist the temptation to draw attention to myself.

But now this need for attention had finally prevailed. I was the rabbi of a major congregation; hundreds of people came to hear me speak every week. I was . . . frequently called upon to speak on ceremonial occasions and at times of public crisis. I had finally given in to my secret desire. . . . All my life I had regarded my need for attention as a terrible defect, an ugly lust. And yet if I hadn't finally managed to get attention focused on me, would I have been able to rally people to protect the homeless or protest the Death Penalty or do any of the things I was proudest of?

We unmask the will of God behind our desires by means of the second stage of spiritual transformation I outlined in the first chapter of this book, in the section entitled "Finding Your Divine Name." The most significant transformation in Jacob's life was when he discovered that the thing he couldn't stand about himself was his divine name: *Yisrael* — "He struggled with God." Like everyone else who knew him, Jacob had always assumed that this tendency to struggle with his lot in life, to strive for something other than what he'd been given, was his worst defect. But when he wrestled with the angel and was renamed Israel, he discovered this tendency was really the source of his unique strength in life — his divine gift. Like Jacob, I also came to the realization that it was precisely the thing I hated about myself that had enabled me to do whatever good I might have managed to do in the world, all the work I thought of as God's work. What I had always regarded as my most neurotic need, a need I had struggled against all my life, had turned out to be my divine name.

This is how we unmask our desires and discover the will of God in them. We cast a mindful eye on our own desires, on our inner darkness, the quality we have come to see as our unique ugliness. The term in the Talmud that most closely expresses the idea of mindfulness is *kavanat lev*, "the directing of the heart." Real mindfulness comes about not by an act of violence against our consciousness, not by trying to forcibly deny or uproot something we find there, not by trying to control our awareness, but rather by a kind of directed compassion, a softening of our awareness, a loving embrace of our life, a soft letting be.

Our impulses, even what seem to be our basest impulses, are divine in origin. Where else could they have come from? The impulse itself is not the problem. The problem is that we have not become mindful of its true nature. We have spent too much time beating ourselves up about it and not enough time holding it in our mindful gaze. The problem is that we have acted on this impulse inappropriately and unconsciously, that we have covered it over with a base human inclination. But the impulse itself is from God. It is what is most meaningful about us; it is what's important, what's holy about us.

In meditation, as we try to focus on the object of our concentration, on the breath and the body, the things we don't like to see about ourselves keep seizing our attention and carrying it away. This is an enormous opportunity. This is a process that gives us the capacity to unmask ourselves and to unmask God at the same time.

PRACTICE POINTS

Listening and Seeing Without Naming

When we sit in meditation, sounds and patterns of light are constantly rising up and falling away in the field of mind. We hear the sound of a car passing by, or a voice, or a bird call, and we say that is a car, that is a person, that is a bird. But if we allow ourselves to listen to the sound itself without attaching a name to it, without giving it form, without reducing it to an idea, we might penetrate to a deeper experience of it; we might enter a deeper and more primal world, a world beyond form.

The sounds that we hear in meditation are the easiest phenomena to work with this way, but by no means the only ones. As we leave the meditation hall and begin to move around the world, either in nature or on the streets of the city, we can continue to practice this kind of primal relationship with our experience; we can let go of the names we usually give to our experience and enter into the experience itself. Out in nature we can stop identifying the objects of our perception as trees and fields and lakes and thereby enter a primary world of color, shape, and pattern. We can do the same on a city street, not saying cars or traffic or stores or pedestrians to ourselves, but just letting these designations go, and inhabiting the jazz-riff patterning they mask.

And this exercise can be applied to the heart as well. Don't name the things you feel. Just feel them. The language you use to describe these feelings is fraught with judgment. Stop beating yourself up for the things you desire. Let your idea of what you feel fall away, and penetrate to the feeling itself.

Spend a few minutes every day not trying to understand what people are saying, but just following their breath as they speak. Spend a few minutes every day ignoring the content, the physicality, of sound and allowing yourself to experience the silence at its center.

The world is far deeper, richer, more mysterious, and more beautiful than you imagine. So stop imagining it. Even just for a few moments a day, inhabit it without giving it a name.

Inhabiting Desire

As we sit in meditation, trying to focus on the breath and the body, thoughts and feelings arise in our mind and heart and eventually we become aware of them. We may, for example, become aware that we want certain things, that we have carnal appetites we were not aware of, the desire to have sex with a particular person, or a free-floating sexual desire with no particular object. Or we may desire to possess something, or to win recognition, approval, fame, or fortune. Our first instinct may be to suppress this desire. Desire is painful. It is painful to want something we don't have and likely never will. So we try to push our desire down, an act that robs us of precious psychic energy and that is futile anyway. The desire will likely keep pushing up to the surface and continue to frustrate us.

Or we may resolve to fulfill our desire. As soon as we are finished meditating, we promise ourselves, we will have that dangerous liaison or go out and spend money we don't have on some obscure object of our longing. Many desires are harmless and their fulfillment perfectly healthy, but others, when we try to act on them, bring immense harm, to ourselves and to others.

In meditation a third approach to desire is available to us. Instead of trying to suppress a desire, or acting on it inappropriately, we can try to inhabit it as thoroughly as we can, to fill it with our awareness, to have the desire itself fill us until we positively bristle with it. We live in a world of perfect economy. Thoughts, impulses, and feelings often arise in our mind because they need to. Often all they need is our attention, a moment of conscious life in our awareness. Suppression and acting out are both strategies for killing off desire, the one by pushing it down, the other by satisfying it and ending it that way. Simply being with our desire is a far less violent and more efficacious strategy. By letting our desire live in the full warmth of our awareness for the brief moment of its rising up, we can actually enjoy it without causing any harm to ourselves or to others. And the desire itself also gets what it needs and happily falls away with the next breath. If it arises again with the breath after that, so be it. We simply inhabit it again, giving it our full attention as we breathe it in, letting it go as we breathe out, neither pushing it down nor pushing it out into the complex and troublesome world of external consequences, but simply being with it for as long as it needs us to be.

Four Worlds in a Half Hour

The journey through the four Kabalistic worlds we described earlier in this chapter can and does take a lifetime to make, but we can also experience it in the space of a single meditation period. Doing so is useful both because it provides us with a map of the larger journey our soul is in the midst of, and because it sensitizes us to the reality that we occupy various realms simultaneously.

We begin in *asiyah*, the realm of materiality, the world of the physical. Here we focus our awareness on the breath and the body, breathing consciously and holding our posture as carefully as we can at the balance point between tension and relaxation, between our rootedness in the earth and our reaching for heaven. (See the practice points at the end of Chapter One for precise details.) When we feel our awareness firmly rooted in this realm — fully planted in the body and the breath — we are ready to move on to the next world.

This is *yetzirah*, the realm of feeling and emotion. Here we shift our focus from the body and endeavor to find a serious answer to Bob Dylan's famous question "How does it feel?" When teaching mindful eating, the Vipassana teacher Sylvia Boorstein suggests that we focus not on the physical sensations of eating — the texture of the food, the way our various teeth work on it, the feel of the food working its way down the esophagus — but rather on the emotional responses it triggers in us. She is describing the shift from *asiyah* to *yetzirah*. After we have saturated the body with awareness, we move on to the heart, the emotional center. We focus on whatever it is we are actually feeling at the moment, be it anger, jealousy, love, regret, desire, or boredom. We enter this emotional state completely, saturating it with awareness, much as we described doing with desire in the last practice point. We inhabit these feelings as thoroughly as we can, and we allow them to enter us. We meet them on the primal level, not as ideas but as full-blown realities as real as our body. After these feelings are bristling in us and our awareness is firmly planted in them, we are ready to move on to *briyah*.

Briyah is the world of conception, of pure thought. The mind is continuously producing thoughts, such an endless and voluminous stream of them, in fact, that it is hard to wrap our awareness around any single thought. Usually we only become aware of thoughts indirectly. We are trying to focus on something else — the breath or the body, or a book we are reading — and thoughts arise and carry our awareness away. When we become aware that this has happened, we also become aware of the thought itself, pure, unconditioned, and unconnected to the kinds of emotional or physical responses our thoughts usually provoke. Conception — thought — is often the basis of both feeling and physical action. It comes first. But there is something that comes before thought too, more basic than thought, although it isn't until we become fully aware of our thoughts that we realize there is something beneath them — prior to them. It is this realization that carries us to the next realm, *atzilut,* the world of pure spiritual emanation.

At the base of thought, before either feeling or physicality, there is a more abstract realm, a world of pure spiritual movement and form, of disembodied light and shape. One of the most interesting possibilities of meditation is that it can carry us to this realm. Recent studies in neurophysics have shown that a few moments before a thought arises, there is a minute discharge of chemical energy in the brain. In meditation (although admittedly, likely not on our first attempt at same) we attend to this moment before thought and experience the energy at its base. Earlier we spoke of how the pain in our leg can be transformed into waves of energy, into a more primal reality. Our thoughts also mask a deeper, more primal reality — a flow of pure spiritual emanation. Great poetry often awakens us to the rhythmic, energetic base of thought. If, as Maimonides claimed, thinking carries us closer to

God, the emanations below the surface of our thinking carry us closer still.

A caveat: This Kabalistic grid of the Four Worlds is a medieval idea. Our medieval ancestors were fascinated by linear hierarchies. As useful as it may be, we should be careful not to take this formulation too seriously. If in the course of our life's path we arrive at the realm of pure thought (*briyah*) before the realm of feeling (*yetzirah*), it's really perfectly all right. The point is to start with the body, and to be aware that we occupy several dimensions at once, and that we are on a journey that constantly carries us from one to another and back and forth between them.

Chapter Seven

Revelation

THE PARTICULAR CIRCUMSTANCES OF A PERSON'S ENLIGHT-
enment determine the nature of the practice he will create as a
teacher. This is a familiar dictum in the Zen world, and the case of
the Bobo Roshi is often cited as an example. "Bobo" is a Japanese
slang word for sexual intercourse. The Bobo Roshi was so named
because of the peculiar lineaments of his enlightenment story. He
had lived in a monastery ever since he was a teenager. Now
approaching the end of middle life, he was beginning to grow discouraged with both his practice and his life. The former had
grown stale and tired and the latter meaningless as a result. Meditation had become painfully routine, and all hopes for satori (Zen
enlightenment) had been long since abandoned. Without knowing it, the Bobo Roshi was well launched into the dark night of the

soul that often precedes enlightenment. Finally he became so discouraged that one night he left the monastery on an impulse, vowing never to return again.

Outside the monastery walls, he had no idea what to do with himself, no plan as to where he might go. He had decided to leave the monastery, but it had never occurred to him to think about what he might do after that. He knew almost nothing of this world from which he had been shielded for most of his life. Presently a prostitute approached him. "Come with me," she said. The Bobo Roshi complied. After all, he had nowhere else to go, nothing else to do. In the prostitute's chambers, he made love to a woman for the first time in his life, and as he reached his first climax, he was engulfed in a kensho — an enlightenment experience — so powerful that the prostitute who lay beneath him became his first disciple.

The Bobo Roshi's enlightenment was affirmed by all the leading masters in Japan, but his career as a teacher was clearly colored by the oddness of his kensho experience. He taught out of a ramshackle house in one of Tokyo's poorer districts, and his students were an odd collection of vagrants, poets, whores, thieves, and madmen. Nor was there much that the Bobo Roshi could do about any of this. He had chosen neither the terms of his enlightenment nor the career it produced. He thought he was quitting the monastery, giving up on his quest for enlightenment altogether, when enlightenment suddenly burst upon him unbidden, as if from beyond.

I often think of this story in terms of my own practice of studying Torah. Succumbing to an overwhelming intuition, my wife and I decided to marry thirteen days after we met. Although neither of us had ever been involved with Judaism much, it was clear from this same blind instinct that we would have to have a Jewish wedding.

The only problem was that we had no connection to any synagogue and we didn't know a single rabbi. We didn't even know where the nearest synagogue might be found. So we turned to the yellow pages and found that the nearest one was a Conservative synagogue in Santa Rosa, California. We called the rabbi and he agreed to see us. He was a charming and charismatic Frenchman named Leo Abrami. As a young Orthodox Parisian he had studied Kabala with some of the finest mystics in Europe. Now his eyes were intense and his hair sprang out of the sides of his head in wiry coils. He agreed to marry us immediately, but I was fascinated by him, and as we sat in his office it began to occur to me that he might be able to help me in other ways as well.

I had recently ended a ten-year practice of Zen Buddhism during which I had meditated for long periods of time every day. Lately I had been missing the daily discipline of this practice a great deal. "Tell me, Rabbi," I said. "When I was a Buddhist, I used to wake up every day at five in the morning and meditate for several hours. Do Jews do anything like that?" "Of course they do," Rabbi Abrami assured me, and then he proceeded to tell me about daily prayer, the donning of phylacteries, and the practice of setting aside a fixed time every morning for the study of Torah. He particularly recommended this last practice to me as a good entryway to Jewish observance. Daily prayer and the wearing of *tefillin* (phylacteries, or scriptural amulets) were a bit opaque and required some preparation and instruction. But I could start studying Torah on my own anytime I wanted, he said. In fact, he recommended a particular format for this practice. Jews all over the world read the same weekly portion of the Torah every week, he said, and each of these portions was divided into seven sections called *aliyot*. Why didn't I read one *aliyah* of the weekly Torah portion every day of the week? This sounded like a good idea, so I commenced doing so the day after our meeting with Rabbi Abrami.

Even though I no longer had a formal relationship with Zen practice, I still meditated first thing every morning. Now I would place a Chumash — a Pentateuch — in front of my meditation cushion, and after a half hour or so of meditation, I would open it and begin to study the *aliyah* appropriate to the day while still in a meditative state. So the study of the Torah began for me as a form of meditation. Words and phrases from the Torah would suddenly assert themselves to me the way thoughts would do in meditation. Passages of Torah, like moments of meditation, would suddenly acquire a vibrance, a radiance; these passages would stay with me all day long, and I would recognize them as I went about my life later in the day. Then eventually the opposite would happen. Moments of life would assert themselves to me during the day, would have a peculiar energy, a radiance about them, and I would find these moments reflected in the Torah as well.

This is still the way I study Torah. The particularity of the circumstances that brought me to Torah determined my practice of Torah as both a teacher and a student forevermore. When I read the Torah, certain passages seem to leap off the page, to possess a certain energy, almost as if the words are covered in light. And there are moments in life that feel the same way, that have an intensity to them that makes them stand out from the generality of life. Also, as in the story of Bobo Roshi, there doesn't seem to be much I can do about any of this. I didn't choose this method of study; it seems to have chosen me.

When Joseph told his family about his dreams of dominance and majesty — all the planets and even the sun and the moon bowed down to him; he bound a great sheaf of wheat and all his brothers' sheaves of wheat bowed down to his — his siblings resented them terribly, says the Bible. *V'aviv shamar et ha-davar* — "but his father remembered the thing." His father, Jacob, felt an intense energy in these dreams, and as a result he knew they were significant, that he would someday recognize them in life. When we pay close attention, we find that there are moments like this in the Torah and moments like this in life — moments that glint at us as if with light — and when we connect them, something extraordinary will often result.

This may seem a little odd — a little at odds with our conventional ideas of study — but I find I am not the first to approach the spiritual discipline of Torah study from this point of view. The Zohar, the classical compendium of Jewish mysticism, tells the following story:

> Human beings are so confused in their minds! They do not see the way of truth in Torah. Torah calls out to them every day in love, but they do not want to turn their heads. Even though I have said that Torah removes a word from her sheath, is seen for a moment then quickly hides away, that is certainly true, but when she reveals herself from her sheath and hides herself right away, she does so only for those who know her intimately.
>
> A parable. To what can the matter be compared? To a lovely princess, beautiful in every way and hidden deep within her palace. She has one lover, unknown to anyone; he is hidden too. Out of his love for her, this lover passes by her gate

constantly, lifting his eyes to every side. She knows that her lover is hovering about her gate constantly. What does she do? She opens a little window in her hidden palace and reveals her face to her lover, then swiftly withdraws, concealing herself. No one near the lover sees or reflects, just the lover, and his heart and his soul and everything within him flows out to her, and he knows that out of love for him, she reveals herself for just that one moment to awaken love in him.

So it is with a word of Torah: she reveals herself to no one but her lover. The Torah knows that he who is wise of heart hovers about her gate every day. What does she do? She reveals herself to him from her palace and beckons him with a hint, then swiftly withdraws to her hiding place. No one who is there knows or reflects; he alone does, and his heart and his soul and everything within him flows out to her. That is why Torah reveals and conceals herself. With love she approaches her lover to arouse love in him.

— *Zohar II, 61.99, translation by Daniel C. Matt*

There is another moment in the Jacob story which once incited this kind of charge in me, which opened its window a little and inflamed me by showing me a little glint of its face. When Jacob returns to confront his brother, Esau, after a sojourn of twenty years in Haran with his uncle Lavan, he sends messengers to Esau and bids them tell him *"im Lavan garti"* — "I have sojourned with Lavan." This phrase, and particularly the word *garti* — "I have sojourned" — had that kind of glint I have been talking about, that sense that the Torah was pulling back a veil and revealing a bit of its radiant face. The word stayed with me all week. I read commentaries on it, but they only succeeded in deepening the mystery. Rashi, for example, pointed out that the word *garti* was an inversion of the word *taryag*, which stands for the number 613. The number 613 has a very powerful valence in the Jewish tradition. The rabbis of the Talmudic and medieval periods employed a complex and often torturous system of exegesis to derive 613 divine commandments from both the narrative and legal portions of the Torah. So according to Rashi, Jacob uses the word *garti* to convey to Esau that even though he has been living with the evil Lavan for all these years, he has managed nevertheless to retain his piety and to observe *taryag* — all 613 commandments of the Torah.

There are several problems with this interpretation, however, not the least of which is that the Torah will not be given to Israel until some four hundred years after Jacob's death, and the rabbinic exegesis that derived the 613 commandments from the Torah would not exist for at least another thousand years after that. Rashi's interpretation of this passage is part of a category of interpretation that has always troubled me. Rashi, and the Talmudic commentators he brings forward, impute an anachronistic piety to the biblical patriarchs, a rigorous observance of Torah in retrograde projection. Neither the Torah nor its Talmudic reformulation has come into existence at the time, yet Abraham, Isaac, and Jacob are all seen as spontaneously following the precepts of this system.

Abraham clearly seems to serve his three divine guests milk and meat together at the terebinths of Mamre, and indeed why shouldn't he? The Torah, which the rabbis claimed (rather dubiously) to outlaw this practice, wouldn't exist for another five hundred years. Yet Rashi goes through contortions to try to explain that Abraham really did separate the milk from the meat when he served his guests food. Why did Abraham wake up early in the morning on the day he was to have bound his son Isaac on the altar for a sacrifice? Not to show his great eagerness to carry out even this most odious divine imperative, as the plain sense of the text seems to suggest, but rather, Rashi insists, to perform the prescribed round of morning prayers.

What was Isaac doing when the Torah describes him as "meditating in the fields" just before he raised his eyes to the horizon and saw his wife-to-be, Rebecca, coming toward him in a caravan of camels? He was performing the prescribed afternoon prayers. Why did Jacob cross the Yabok River late at night so that he could be alone there? So that he could say the prescribed evening prayers. Never mind that none of these prayer services would be prescribed at all for another fifteen hundred years.

So what was Rashi getting at here? Rashi, after all, was no dope, but a great religious genius. He knew perfectly well when the patriarchs lived, when the Torah was given, and when the rabbinic exegesis of the Torah took place. So what was he getting at when he brought forward these interpretations that seemed to fly in the face of simple common sense? What had begun as a barely perceptible glint of light over the Hebrew word *garti* had evolved into a kind of koan — a question that defied a logical answer — which haunted me all week long.

At the end of that week I had to drive to Los Angeles to participate in the Second International Conference on Jewish Meditation. What was Jewish meditation? Was there a really a tradition of meditation in Judaism, and if not, was there really anything particularly Jewish about meditation itself? None of this was very clear, but there were suddenly thousands of Jews practicing meditation in Jewish contexts all over the world. These were the kinds of questions we had debated endlessly the previous year at the first such conference, which had been held in my own synagogue in San Francisco. Now, in Los Angeles, the argument would no doubt continue along similar lines.

I was scheduled to speak at the conference early Sunday morning, but I had to preside over a bar mitzvah that weekend, so I couldn't begin driving until late Saturday night after the Sabbath. The feeling of Shabbat was still quite strong as I got into the car, and I was listening to some tapes of Hasidic music that only deepened this sense as I drove on into the night. The hour grew later and later, and I fell into a kind of state — almost a trance — and as I hurtled through San Luis Obispo at around three in the morning, the answer to the great koan posed by Rashi's interpretation of the word *garti* came to me in a flash. Suddenly I realized that when you truly entered the great stream of spiritual consciousness from which the Jewish people had been addressing God for the past several thousand years, time ceased to flow in only one way. Every point in that stream was connected to every other point and partook of it. So that when the rabbis of the Middle Ages began to prescribe the morning prayer service, Abraham, who was in their blood and their DNA, but more significantly, in this stream with them, also prayed the morning service and had always done so. And Isaac *davened mincha* — prayed the prescribed service of the afternoon — because he was also in the stream with them, and prayed when they prayed. And so on. Time flows in every direction in this great stream. Those who enter it do what those who were already there did, and those who were there from the beginning take on the practices of those who came after them.

So it was, I explained to the conference later that morning in Los Angeles, that when I assumed the lotus position to meditate every day, Abraham also crossed his legs. But only to the degree that I was in the stream; only to the degree that I had given myself to Jewish spiritual consciousness; only to the degree that I practiced it every day and thus became part of it; only to the degree that its koans became my koans. On the deepest level, I explained, this was how meditation became Jewish meditation. And on that bright but blurry morning in Los Angeles, the truth of what I was saying seemed self-evident both to me and to everyone present. And it had all begun with a barely perceptible glimmer of light around the word *garti*.

What was also apparent was how little control I had exerted over the process of extracting meaning from this word. Like the princess opening the little window in her tower, this word had insinuated itself to me of its own accord. Nor had I had much to do with the answer suddenly bursting upon me as I barreled through San Luis Obispo. Torah, like koan study, often reveals itself to us precisely when we come to the limits of our own powers, our capacity to coerce an answer from it by dint of our rationality. This insight had seemed to come upon me from the outside, first as a glimmer of light from the Torah and then as an explosion of it.

Sometimes the glimmer of light begins in life and ends up in the Torah. Toward the end of the Joseph narrative, it is finally revealed to Joseph's brothers that the Egyptian prince who has been tormenting them is really their brother Joseph, whom they threw into a pit and then sold into slavery to a band of Midianites bound for Egypt. Naturally they are terrified that Joseph will now take revenge on them, but Joseph seeks to reassure them.

> "I am your brother Joseph whom you **sold** into Egyptian slavery. But now, don't be sad and don't be afraid because you **sold** me thusly, because God **sent** me here before you to save life; God **sent** me here before you to preserve a remnant in the land, to give life to a great remainder. And now [you must know] it wasn't you who **sent** me here, but rather, it was God." [Emphasis added.]

Nechama Leibowitz, the great modern Torah commentator, notes the juxtaposition of the words "sold" and "sent" in this passage. "The two different facets of the deed are here placed side by side, or rather in sequence; the deed as it appeared superficially and its deeper implications," Leibowitz writes. "On the surface, to the eye, it appeared a sale. But on a deeper insight, a mission was revealed."

The brothers sold Joseph to Egypt. It was they who threw him into the pit, and they have to take responsibility for this misdeed. In fact, on the deep unconscious level of this text, we see them working out their repentance for it — burning off their karma, as it were. According to Maimonides, this story is the purest example we have of Teshuvah Gemorah — of complete and perfect repentance. We see the brothers brought to the exact same moment with Benjamin they had earlier faced with Joseph; their younger, favored brother was in a pit again, and it was in their power to save him. They had willfully chosen to let Joseph be carried off to a life of subjugation, but now, at the risk of his own life,

Judah steps forward and attempts to save Benjamin. So while there is no absolution for their sin, epitomized here by the word "sold," there is repentance for it, and more significantly, there is the assertion that even in their sinning, they were carrying out a providential mission. They were instruments of the divine will; their actions, however execrable they may have been, served the larger purpose of saving many lives, and of carrying forward the historical destiny of their people.

So as Joseph's speech goes on, the verb "sold," the selfish, wrongheaded behavior all of us engage in, gives way to "sent," the divine mission even our worst behavior helps to carry forward. This change in language brings about a corresponding change in the way we understand the events of the world. There is the immediate cause of things — the chain of causality that plays itself out on the surface of the world — and then there is the deeper cause, the one we seldom see or understand, but that often redeems the first.

Maimonides addresses this phenomenon in the *Guide to the Perplexed.*

It is clear that everything produced must have an immediate cause which produced it; that cause again, a cause and so on until the First Cause, i.e., the will and decree of God is reached. The prophets, therefore, sometimes omit the intermediate causes and ascribe the production of an individual thing directly to God saying that God has made it, God has done it, commanded it, said it or sent it. [This is true] regarding phenomena produced regularly by natural causes such as the melting of snow when the atmosphere becomes warm, the roaring of the sea when a storm rages etc. and it is also true of events caused by man's free will such as war, the dominion of one nation over another, the attempt of one person to hurt another or to insult him.

Maimonides adduces many examples from the Bible, including the present passage, when Joseph declares, "It wasn't you who sent me here, but rather, it was God." In other words, each of us sees the immediate implications and motivations of our own behavior. We imagine we are carrying out our own set purposes without understanding the force of the divine will our behavior carries forward.

But I am presenting all this to you backwards, because on the week in question, the glimmer of light that sensitized me to all this appeared not in the Torah, but rather in the world, in my life. Only later did the Torah affirm what I had glimpsed there.

My mother had been visiting me from New York that week. As much as I loved her and loved to spend time with her, there was a great sadness in seeing her. My mother has Alzheimer's disease, and in those days, when the disease was still in its earlier stages, there was a sense of decline — of the relentless progression of the disease, of her helplessly slipping into oblivion — every time I saw her. She still knew us then. She still had a general sense of who and where she was, but each time I saw her, it was clear that she had lost another big chunk of vocabulary, another big chunk of memory and understanding.

This sense of her relentlessly slipping away and my own impotence in the face of her illness was exacerbated by both her arrival in and her departure from San Francisco. Traveling was especially difficult and fearful for her then. She could never remember what arrangements had been made, so after she had been put on the plane, she was never sure who, if anyone, would be waiting for her at the other end of her journey. For this reason we were always very careful to come to the airport on time, realizing how terrifying it would be for her to arrive and not find anyone waiting for her. So on the day when her plane was due in San Francisco, I called the airport several times and was told that her flight would come in right on time. But just to make sure, I got to the airport forty-five minutes early, only to find my mother waiting for me, terrified, having no idea where she was or who was supposed to meet her. Her flight, it seems, had arrived an hour and a half early. Talk about impotence and helplessness! Here I had done everything in my power to prevent exactly what had occurred: I had called the airport several times (remember the old Shelley Berman line: "If your child is a compulsive liar, don't worry; he can always get a very good job working for the airlines"), and I had arrived at the airport quite early, yet the very thing I had feared had happened.

My mother stayed in San Francisco for ten days and we had a lovely visit, but her departure was marred by a similar incident. I took her to the airport and asked the man at the gate if I could walk her onto the plane and get her settled in her seat. This was against the rules, of course, but in the more relaxed days before 9/11, they usually let me do it anyway. But this time they didn't; they stuck to the rules.

"She gets very confused," I explained. "I'm worried that she'll get on the plane and won't know where she is and won't be able to find her seat."

"Don't worry," the man said. "I'll walk her onto the plane myself."

So he did. I saw him walk her into the cabin of the plane and come out five or ten minutes later. I wanted to wait in the boarding area until the plane had actually left the ground. The worst catastrophe, of course, would be that they would find something wrong with the plane and ask everyone to get off and plop my mother down in the middle of a strange airport again with no one to take care of her. But once the plane left the boarding gate, it was hard to tell if it had taken off or not. I went to the boarding desk and explained the situation.

"What's your mother's name?" the woman there asked me.

"Charlotte Lew," I told her.

"Oh yes," she said. "We had a lot of trouble with her. When she got on the plane she didn't know where to sit, and she couldn't remember what she had done with her boarding pass. We finally had to come outside and look her up on the computer. I wish we had known she had someone here."

Apparently the charming fellow who had offered to walk her onto the plane had done just that. He had walked her on and then left her there to fend for herself. He hadn't even taken her to her seat. Once again the very situation I had been trying to avoid had taken place. In spite of my best efforts to control the situation, my mother had been left on her own in a strange place, terrified and bewildered. These incidents just seemed to encapsulate the nightmare of my mother's condition — the helplessness we all felt as she slowly slipped out of our grasp — and to evoke an even deeper sense of impotence concerning life in general. How little we seem to be able to control after all, I thought. We expend our life energy trying to get our children to become what we think they should be, and they turn into something else altogether. We work and work, weekends and evenings, but still feel unappreciated or undone by our own unconscious compulsions. In the words of the Indian mystic Kabir, "Everything you do has some weird failure in it."

I began the drive home from the airport with tears in my eyes — tears of rage and frustration to be sure, but also tears of simple grief. Then on Highway 280 just south of the city, I saw something truly miraculous that somehow healed me of these feelings. It was a scene worthy of an Eisenstein movie. All three oncoming lanes were clogged full of cars backed up and sitting still for what seemed like miles. The line stretched all the way back to the city. There at the head of this logjam was a terrible accident, two cars on the side of the road, both of them apparently totaled. There were ambulances and police cars all around. An accident victim was being lifted from one of the cars and put into an ambulance.

And here is the moment that healed me. There must have been eight men around that stretcher, big burly cops and ambulance drivers, but they were lifting that stretcher with an incredible delicacy. You could see on their faces and by the way they held their hands that they were aware of what a precious and fragile burden they were carrying, what a sacred thing — a human being, a human life. You could see the wonder and the concern in those big burly faces, and suddenly you could see it in the entire scene stretching before your eyes. You could see it in all the hundreds of cars that had stopped on the freeway behind this accident, in this long line of traffic stretching back for miles. How sacred was this life? So sacred that all these cars would stop to honor the delicacy — the tenuousness — of this moment.

Suddenly I realized I was watching an immense pageant, a pageant to the sanctity of life, a pageant directed by God. Few if

any of the people in all those cars realized that they were participating in this pageant. Most of them had no idea why the traffic
had come to a standstill or that they were waiting for a life to be
saved, waiting while eight burly men inched forward toward the
ambulance with their precious burden. The people in the cars had
their own purposes for being on Highway 280 that day. They
thought they were on the way to the airport or to the Serramonte
Shopping Center or to work. Each had his own particular understanding of the implications of what was going on: I will be late;
I am sitting here stewing because the car ahead of me is sitting
there stewing, because the car ahead of him is sitting there stewing, and so on into infinity. They had no idea they were serving a
larger purpose at the moment, that God was employing them to
express that life is so precious that all activity — even the progress
of hundreds of cars on the freeway — must come to a complete
stop if even one life is in peril. They may have set out onto Highway 280 to exchange a Hanukkah present at Macy's Serramonte;
they may have begun with "sold," but beneath that was "sent";
God had sent them to express some larger purpose.

And that's why I was healed of the grief and impotence I had
felt concerning my mother at the airport. We all see the immediate implications of our actions. Sometimes we feel in control of
our lives, but most of the time they seem to be spinning out of
control. But what both the Joseph story and our own lives suggest
is that someone, something, is in control. We imagine we are trying to carry out our own purposes, but without our realizing it, our
lives become subsumed in a larger purpose.

At the very beginning of the Joseph story, when Jacob first
sends Joseph to meet his brothers in Dotan — where they will

throw him into the pit and then sell him into slavery in Egypt, where he will save many lives and change the entire course of human history — the Torah tells us, "And he sent him from the valley [*emek*] of Hebron," a wonderfully ambiguous line. Who sent Joseph, Jacob or God? Jacob imagined that he was only sending Joseph to spend a few days with his brothers; he had no idea that this sending was part of the divine mission to save life and to fulfill the destiny of a people.

What is the meaning of the word *emek*? As Rashi points out, the word has a double meaning here. It means "valley," but it also means "a place of great depth and mystery." Every moment of our lives has such a double meaning. Every step we take has the meaning we imagine it has and a deeper, more mysterious meaning as well. Every action we take flows out of our own motivation and into an intentionality beyond our own. When we really understand this, despair seems so unnecessary and our need to control things so irrelevant.

Every moment of life, every word of the Torah, is charged with meaning; every moment, every word, is brimming with light. If we love life, if we love Torah, if we live life and live Torah in a disciplined and mindful fashion, if we pass by her gate constantly, lifting our eyes to every side, she will reveal herself to us for a moment. She will open a little window in her hidden palace, and we will see a numinous glint of light, and our heart and our soul and everything within us will flow out to her, because we know that she has only shown us this light out of love for us, and to arouse love in us. We are not in control of this process. It happens of its own accord. If we see the light in our lives, it will be illuminated in the Torah as well. If the Torah opens a small window in

the secret palace it is hiding in, if one of its words or phrases suddenly takes on a surprising and unreasonable intensity, we can be
sure that we will also see this light reflected in our life. So it is that
we come not so much to understand life, but to feel its supernal
depths, to feel the profound meaning and mystery that inform it.

PRACTICE POINTS

Torah Study: Listening for the Voice of God

Set aside a fixed time for study every day. Not necessarily a lot of
time, nor a lot of study, but the important thing is that it be regular
and fixed; in short, a practice. In my experience Torah study is not
like other forms of reading. In Torah study we are aware of the
process of reading itself. We are aware, for example, that when we
read, our mind often wanders. We may get stuck on a particular
passage for half an hour. We may read the same sentence over and
over again a hundred times before we even realize what we are
doing. Then suddenly a word or a phrase or a sentence or a page
will leap up at us and catch our attention. Our mind will be suddenly awake and focused on what we are reading. In Torah study
both the passages that catch our attention and the passages that
set us off on a long rumination are significant. They are God
speaking to us through the text of the Torah. The practice of
Torah study is the practice of hearing that voice.

Or we may simply notice that certain words or phrases or
sentences in the text are charged as though lit from within. And
we may notice moments in our life like that as well. When we put
the charged words or phrases or sentences together with the
charged moments, we might find a significant rhyme, we might

find that one instructs us about the other, and that both taken together are extremely significant for us, telling us something we really needed to know.

The practice is simply to be consistently aware — of the Torah, of the process of reading it, of our life. These are not different things.

Some practical advice: Torah study is a communal activity. The Torah is read every year in a cycle of weekly portions, and Jews all around the world read the same portion every week. Studying Torah in this cycle gives one a sense of being in tune with a kind of global spiritual momentum. There is the additional advantage, of course, of never having to worry about where to start, what to read, or when to read it. All Jewish calendars (available in Jewish bookstores, funeral parlors, food stores, and so on) indicate which portion is read in a given week, and all Chumashim (Pentateuchs — the five books of Moses) are organized according to these weekly portions. The most popular American Pentateuchs are *The Pentateuch and Haftorahs,* edited by J. H. Hertz; *Etz Hayim: Torah and Commentary,* edited by David Leiber; and *Torah: A Modern Commentary,* edited by Gunther Plaut. Each weekly portion is divided into seven sections called *aliyot.* If you wish to follow the practice described earlier in the chapter of reading a single *aliyah* every day of the week, you may need some help in identifying these *aliyot* from a rabbi or other knowledgeable Jew. Most Chumashim only indicate these divisions on the Hebrew side, and even then, only subtly.

I used to keep a Chumash by the side of my meditation cushion every day and read the appropriate *aliyah* after a forty-minute period of meditation. It might work better for you to sit in a chair or to have a shorter period of meditation before the reading.

The important point is to have some period of contemplation before the reading so that you are sensitive to the more subtle forms of communication the Torah employs — not just the meaning of the words, but also the charge around them. It may take some time to attune yourself to this kind of material. Be like a hunter stalking prey (or like that lover constantly passing by the princess's gate). It may take many days of waiting and watching before the deer appears or the window flashes open for a moment. Or in Whitman's words, "Failing to fetch me at first keep encouraged, / Missing me one place search another, / I stop somewhere waiting for you."

Chapter Eight

The Overflowing Cup

Yitzchak Abravanel, the great fifteenth-century Spanish Torah commentator, saw the Torah as describing a complete spiritual journey, with each of its five books representing a distinct stage in this journey.

The first of these books, the book of Genesis, begins with the creation of all humankind but then quickly funnels down to the particularity of individual human beings, the members of a single family. It describes the individual spiritual path in the lives of Abraham, Isaac, and Jacob, of Sarah, Rebecca, Rachel, and Leah — their twists and turns, their sufferings and their vicissitudes, all of it quite recognizable to us from our own lives. Genesis is concerned with the personal spiritual journey, with all its leave-takings and the encounters with the transcendent that these leave-takings engender.

Exodus shows how our personal journey is subsumed into the journey of our people; the family we encountered in the first book has now become a nation, a distinct spiritual community. This entire community now experiences a leave-taking, the exodus from Egypt, and a consequent revelation, the giving of the Torah on Mount Sinai.

No sooner does this theophany take place than the Children of Israel come to understand that if this revelation is going to resonate in their lives, they will need a practice, a sacred space, and a body of ritual to both contain and express the seminal revelation they received on Mount Sinai. In fact this insight is itself a part of the revelation. So the second half of the book of Exodus and the entire book of Leviticus are entirely given over to the building of a sacred space and to the cultivation of the spiritual practice that will take place in it: the Tabernacle the Children of Israel will carry through the wilderness and the sacrificial cult they will practice in it. The Tabernacle is, in effect, a portable Mount Sinai, and the spiritual practice it houses endeavors to re-create the intimacy with God that was felt at Sinai.

Skipping ahead for a moment, the fifth book, Deuteronomy, is concerned with the reflection that comes before death, Moses's personal iteration of the events presented previously by an omniscient narrator. It also serves as a significant fulcrum for Israel's transition out of the desert and into the Promised Land.

But it is in the fourth book, the book of Numbers, that the rubber really hits the road. This book, which describes the forty years of wandering in the wilderness, addresses the most important question on the spiritual path: How do we make the crucial transition from spiritual practice to daily living? How do we bring our practice into life, so that our life is transformed by the revelation our practice has carried forward? How do we bring our spiritual practice out of the sanctuary and into the wilderness we are trying to cross?

Numbers begins with the elaborate arrangement of the Israelites' camp in preparation for their great march through the wilderness. The Israelites will march with the Tabernacle, the locus of practice, at their center. The last half of Exodus and all of Leviticus describe a world of almost perfect order and harmony. The rituals are described in great and loving detail, as if performed in some cosmic realm apart from life. But in the book of Numbers, the narrative resumes. After carefully arraying themselves around the Tabernacle, the Israelites continue on their march toward the Promised Land, and as they do, all the messiness and disorder of actual life resurface. The Israelites complain about the food. They complain about the water. They fall into bouts of false nostalgia for their lives as slaves in Egypt, suffer a disastrous failure of nerve on the brink of the Promised Land, and rebel against Moses. They experience irrational anger, jealousy, failure, and death. In short, they experience life, but all the while the Tabernacle is still at their center. They are still carrying it around with them. The Torah has delineated their practice in a removed and antiseptic realm: in the realm of the ideal. Here in the book of Numbers, we see them wrestling with a pivotal question: How do we do this practice in the midst of the real? How do we bring our spiritual practice into our actual lives?

This is the question that remains after our personal journey, its attendant crises and defeats, its rocks and hard places, has brought us to the point of a significant departure from the life we have been living, and to the hard-won illuminations that come as a result. And this is the question that remains after we have taken on a spiritual practice to replicate this leave-taking and its resultant revelation. It is the crucial question of the spiritual enterprise, the question without which the entire endeavor has no meaning. How do we make this transition? How does our life become an expression of our practice?

Some years ago my wife and I found ourselves locked in a life-and-death struggle with our fifteen-year-old daughter. She was staging a full-scale rebellion against our authority as parents. She had dropped out of school and run away from home several times. We spent most of that year holding on for dear life, trying to exert leverage on her, to force her to live the way we thought she should live, and failing miserably. Near-violent confrontations, heart-rending anxiety, and an almost suicidal desperation on our part were the order of the day. The police couldn't help us, nor could an endless succession of therapists. The good ones managed to keep things relatively cool between us, and the ones who weren't so good only managed to make matters worse. People advised us to have her kidnapped and sent away to one of those boot camps for wayward teens in the mountains of Utah, or to have her declared an emancipated minor and throw her on the mercy of the courts, but we just couldn't bring ourselves to do these things.

What finally began to turn things around was that after a year or so, my wife and I began to realize that this was also practice. Letting go of our idea of how things should be and meeting what actually arose with compassionate attention was not just something we did when we sat with our legs crossed early in the morning in the meditation hall; it was a way to live, and it was the answer to our problem with our daughter. For many months we let go of all ideas of how our daughter should be and focused on affirming how she actually was, on loving her as she was. It was difficult and required all our attention, but after several months she began to come around, and now, years later, she is as loving and as productive as she was hostile and self-destructive back then. But what amazes me most about this period, looking back on it, is how long it took me to recognize that I needed to apply the principles of the spiritual discipline I had been practicing to this life circumstance, how long it took me to act on the principle that my practice was also about my life.

This is an absolutely crucial leap on the spiritual path, and like all significant leave-takings, it's one we usually take only when we have to, when our backs are to the wall and we have no choice but to leap or perish. But when such desperate moments come, spiritual practice really proves its worth. Suffering and difficulty do not always bring enlightenment in their wake; they are just as likely to crush us, to leave us broken and paralyzed with bitterness and regret. But if we have a daily, disciplined spiritual practice that helps us to give up our ideas of how things should be and to be lovingly present with whatever arises, this inclination is likely to eventually spill over from our practice to our lives, and even the most intractable problems will begin to give way.

One Shabbat afternoon at Mincha, the afternoon prayer service, after a twenty-four-hour retreat consisting of meditation, prayer, Torah study, and long, festive meals spent in silence except for the singing of *niggunim* (wordless chants) and *zemirot* (table songs), we were chanting the Twenty-third Psalm, a tradition at the last hours of Shabbat. A line of the psalm kept asserting itself to me: "My cup flows over [*Cosi revaiyah*]. Surely goodness and kindness pursue me all the days of my life [*cal yamei chayai*], and

I will live in the house of God [*shavti b'vait Yud-hey-vuv-hey*] for the length of my days."

These three Hebrew phrases seemed to be enveloped in the kind of intensity I described in the last chapter — that radiance that signals me that the words or phrases in question have something profound to communicate to me. In this case the message seemed to be an answer to the question we just posed. How do we bring our practice to daily life?

Here's how we do it: Every day of our life, as we meditate, we engage in the exercise of inhabiting the house of God — of *Yud-heh-vuv-heh*, of being in the present tense, of absolute becoming, past, present, and future — until we have saturated the present moment of our life with consciousness. Then *cosi revaiyah*, this consciousness spills over from the act of meditation itself into our daily activities.

When we first practice meditation or any kind of spiritual exercise, we are usually drawn to the epiphanies, the spectacular eruptions of inner light and energy that often accompany such activity, particularly when it is still new. It takes a long time to learn to distinguish between cosmic effulgence and gastric distress (and to learn that they are of about equal significance), or to learn that those spectacular sunbursts or spiraling op art patterns we see when we first close our eyes in meditation are just the way the light looks through the tissue of our eyelids or the skittish disclosures of a nervous system not used to being watched.

When we begin to figure all this out, we either quit and go on to some other form of cheap entertainment or we accept that real spiritual practice is not about pyrotechnics, but about the grinding dailiness of our lives — the daily dream we sleepwalk through, the daily sense of disconnection we feel from ourselves, from others, from our experience, and from God, the unconscious impulses that hold us in their thrall every day.

Mindlessness is a habit with tremendous gravitational force. There are few things as obstinate in this world as "the uncircumcised heart," a redolent biblical phrase for that state of denial, that unawakened state, we occupy most of the time. The inertia of this state is almost irresistible.

If we are to have any chance at all of overcoming these very powerful entropic forces, we need to establish a countervailing inertia of equal force, and this we can only do by daily practice. The only way we can establish the habit of mindfulness and open our heart to the reality of our experience and to God, who is embedded in its moment-by-moment unfolding, is by establishing a daily practice wherein we saturate the present moment with awareness. We live in the house of God, the present moment, and then we let that awareness spill over into the realms of our daily experience.

This is why every spiritual tradition worth its salt stresses the necessity of disciplined, daily practice. Only something we do every day (*cal yamei chayai*) has the power to transform us. Retreats and workshops make good reinforcements for daily practice, but they are no substitute for it. Judaism is primarily a discipline that endeavors to imbue every moment of our lives with a sense of the transcendent. We can't simply bring mindfulness to our daily life by an act of will, by just deciding we'll be more mindful in our daily life and expecting it to happen. But there are many things we can do.

We can, for instance, spend time every day saturating the body and the breath with mindfulness, until our sense of these most fundamental aspects of our present-tense experience gradually becomes vibrant and radiant. Then this vibrant, radiant sense of things spills over into our daily life and we find ourselves inhabiting a vibrant, radiant world, a sacred world, a world suffused with the presence of God. And we find ourselves exclaiming like Jacob, "*Achen, yesh Adonai ba-makom hazeh v'anochi lo yadati*" — "God was in this very place all along and I didn't know it."

We can saturate our physicality with awareness. We can sit planted in the earth with our head reaching for heaven (*mutzav artzah v'rosho magia ha-shamaimah*), until the divine impulses (*malachei Elohim*) that are constantly rising and falling in the mind — thoughts, feelings, energies, and of course the breath itself — begin to come clearly into focus. Or in the language of the Kabala, we can saturate the world of materiality (*asiyah*) with awareness and then let this awareness spill over into the realm of feeling (*yetzirah*), and then pure thought (*briyah*), and then, finally, pure spiritual emanation (*atzilut*).

We can become aware of the thoughts and impulses that carry us away from whatever we are trying to focus on in meditation. The moment we do that is probably the most important moment in meditation, because if we witness this happening every day, we begin to become conscious of our unconsciousness. We begin to see what we have been reluctant or have refused to see, and these things are invariably important; they are the unconscious impulses that shape our behavior. When we witness their rising up and falling away every day, we begin to disarm them. Our awareness of them begins to spill over from the act of meditation — from attending to that moment — to our daily life, and these unconscious patterns begin to lose their power to shape our responses to life. We become less inclined to oppress ourself, or inflict hurt on others inadvertently.

We can also allow the vibrant, awakened sense that comes from saturating the present moment with awareness to spill over into normative Jewish spiritual practices. The elements of ordinary Jewish spiritual practice — daily prayer, the study of Torah, the serious observance of Shabbat — are not problematic spiritual forms. The problem is that we have been sleepwalking through them. Judaism — normative, traditional Judaism — is a spiritual practice of great depth and integrity. But by and large it has been discarded in this century by American Jews, who ironically often complain that Judaism is lacking in spirituality and frequently look elsewhere for spiritual gratification. I think that if Judaism is going to survive in this country, it will be because it will have succeeded in retrieving this sense of itself as a practice — not as an ethnicity, not as an occasional church — but as a set of intentional and disciplined gestures that have the effect of transforming us, of deepening our relationship to the sacred.

I have been practicing Jewish daily prayer for more than twenty-five years now. When I daven each morning at minyan, I often daydream through the service. Many times nothing happens at all. I have been meditating for over thirty years, and I often daydream through that as well. Sometimes nothing happens there either.

But at least once each morning at minyan, a word or a phrase from the prayer service will suddenly sneak up on me and burst into significance, suddenly assert itself and rise up out of the jumble of sounds, the way a particular sound or sensation can race to the foreground of consciousness during meditation. Phrases will divorce themselves from their obvious contexts and take on a new meaning altogether, or they will seem to be speaking directly to me. Each day it will be a different word, a different phrase, and it will stay with me all day. And as I go about my life, I will see its meaning permutating, shedding unexpected light on my life and lending it depth and density. One day last week it was the phrase *karov Adonai lishburei lev* — "God is close to the brokenhearted" — and as I went through the day I was keenly aware of a sense of the sacred hovering over the brokenhearted as they came in for counseling, or when I visited them in the hospital, or when I saw them standing on the highway dividers begging for money. The week before that another phrase had leapt up and grabbed my attention — *ci hitzalti nafshi mi mavet, et ragli medechi,* "because you saved my soul from death and my legs from stumbling" — and all day long I walked around with a palpable sense of what a miracle it was that my life was being sustained and that one foot knew to step in front of the other.

But this is only to speak of the verbal aspects of the act of prayer. In my experience, even though it uses language as its medium, prayer is essentially a nonverbal spiritual discipline. The great rush of words (I don't mind that we pray as quickly as we do) works as a kind of antilanguage. It wipes my mind clean of language and conceptual thought. Daveners who have had strokes that affect their ability to speak, write, and read are still able to daven because prayer comes from the nonverbal center of the brain. Its essential gesture is to concentrate on the text of the *siddur,* the prayer book. Inevitably your mind is carried off by thoughts and distractions, and when you become aware that this has happened, you gently bring your mind back to the object of its focus. As in meditation, it is this gentle bringing back to focus, rather than the words of the *siddur* — the objects of focus themselves — that lies at the heart of the spiritual discipline of daily prayer.

The prayer service uses language, but it describes an essentially nonverbal event, an exchange of pure energy. I often feel this most intensely during the Amidah, the centerpiece of the service. During the Amidah we pray for various personal concerns — health, material well-being, spiritual redemption — and toward the end we also pray that our prayers will be heard and that God will respond to them. Standing silently with my hands clasped to my chest, I often feel that these prayers are ascending and descending like the angels on Jacob's ladder, divine energy coming down to heal and redeem us, a divine consciousness to meet the energy of our voices, our prayers, and our spirits as we raise them to heaven. Sometimes all content, all imagery, verbal or otherwise, will fade away altogether, and I will feel myself to be in the presence of a formless transcendent radiance, which I take to be the presence of God.

The Amidah begins by invoking the names of my ancestors, pointing me away from my identity as a discrete ego and toward something larger — that stream of spiritual consciousness from which we have been addressing God for several thousand years, and which we join when we say these prayers. I often feel that all the people who have used these words with heart and sincerity for all these thousands of years have insinuated themselves into them. When I say them myself, I am with them in that stream of words which derive tremendous sanctity from the souls who have poured themselves into them.

Even before reciting the Amidah, one takes three steps backward and then forward again, in a gesture that came from the ancient protocol for approaching a king. This stepping forward and back is a physical reinforcement of the belief that one is entering another space, a sacred space in which one can encounter God.

This is not just an idea; it has a physical reality. It is something we do with our bodies. We don't just try to connect with God with our minds and our souls, we bind ourselves to the name of God with leather strips through the practice of wearing phylacteries, or *tefillin*. The prayer service is full of gesture: we bow, we stand, we sit, we cover our eyes, we kiss the fringes of our prayer shawl. The discipline of Jewish prayer has a powerful physical dimension, a physical sense of encounter with the transcendent, and this sense of encounter often remains with me all day long.

Later in the day, if I am feeling particularly desperate or for some other reason am in urgent need of communing with God, I go back to my *makom kavuah* (literally, my "fixed place"), the spot in the synagogue from which I pray every day. Precisely because I address God from that spot every day, because I encounter the transcendent from that spot so often, when I return there later in the day, the associations I feel — the way the light hits my eyes, the way the air feels, all the feelings my body experiences in that particular setting — immediately put me in a frame of mind conducive to encountering the transcendent. In fact the encounter begins as soon as I stand in that spot. And the longer this practice goes on, the more days and months and years I pray from that spot, the deeper this encounter gets, the deeper the original feeling, and the associations with it, and the more they stay with me as I go about my life.

The same is true of Shabbat. When I first began to observe Shabbat, I was very much taken in by the pyrotechnics of it, which are, in fact, quite strong. There is a powerful feeling of peace and well-being that results from the kind of withdrawal from the world Shabbat offers us. There is an infectious joyousness to the Shabbat services, especially the Kabbalat Shabbat, the exuberant service with which we greet the onset of the Sabbath. But as time goes on, these pyrotechnics become more difficult to sustain. They are, after all, a sign of the novelty of the experience, something we are much more likely to feel early on as the differential between observing Shabbat and not doing so. After a while we might find ourselves expressing a forced sense of exuberance and joy, and what we first experienced as peace and well-being may give way to simple boredom. But if we persevere through this phase and continue observing Shabbat, we may eventually find that Shabbat has altered the deep structure of our consciousness, of our mind and soul; it has implanted the rhythm of the cosmos there — the alternation of stasis and motion, of activity and rest, of rising up and falling away.

We feel these things in macrocosm when we meditate; we experience this rhythmic alteration every time we take a conscious breath in and then out again. But Shabbat imposes the same structure onto the larger arc of our life, so that we understand that we participate in it, both in the moment-by-moment rising up and falling away of our lives with each breath, and in the fact that we ourselves will fall away one day. We were born and we will die, and this is the natural order of things and not something to be feared. We learn this from a conscious apprehension of the moment-by-moment course of our respiration, and from this weekly withdrawal from work and activity as well. Many of us are driven to lives of ceaseless activity by a deep fear of stillness and the intimation of the great stillness at the end of life it carries with it. Shabbat enables us to befriend this stillness, to see that it doesn't threaten us after all, but is simply part of the natural rhythm of our lives.

There is a considerable liberation in this leave-taking, but only when we practice it in a disciplined fashion. From the outside, people often take the restrictions of Shabbat to be confining and oppressive. From the inside, however, they have precisely the opposite effect. Refraining from working, traveling, shopping, doing business of any kind, cooking, and even carrying objects in public places leaves one feeling immensely free. One feels free from the burden of having to do these things and free of the habits of ordinary life. Discarding the forms that ordinarily hold us in their thrall, we penetrate to the powerful emptiness at the center of our experience; doing nothing, we experience the nothingness beyond all forms, that charged state beyond definition or utterance which gives meaning to our activities.

At Makor Or, the meditation center Norman Fischer and I established adjacent to my synagogue in San Francisco, we have found Shabbat and meditation to be a particularly powerful combination. We have always done meditation before our Shabbat services, both Friday night and Saturday morning, but we often hold meditation retreats on Shabbat as well, filling in all the spaces between prayer, Torah study, and communal meals with extended periods of sitting meditation. The two disciplines reinforce each other powerfully. In meditation we leave our ordinary unconscious state and enter a state of mindful focus where we breathe in, let go of the breath, and breathe in again. Our mind continually produces forms that cause us to suffer, and we continually let go of these forms and return to our awareness of the breath, an awareness that connects us to the Ain Sof, the powerful emptiness at the root of existence.

Shabbat builds this same dynamic into the larger arc of our life. *Shavat vayinafash* — Stop and breathe again, stop and reensoul yourself, the Torah admonishes. On Shabbat we stop acting and we fall into a deep state of being; we cease all activity that involves the creation of forms and we breathe; we connect with the deeper, more primal reality beneath the ceaseless swirl of activity and form. We stop and we do nothing for twenty-five hours, and as the content of our lives falls away, time thickens and takes on depth. Our relationships deepen as well. Our lives become thick and rich. A sense of wholeness begins to emerge out of this nothingness, this nondoing. We fall silent and stop drowning out God's music. We do nothing, yet the world sustains us anyway, instilling a deep confidence in us. We become still, and for the rest of the week our activity seems to arise out of this stillness with a sense of inevitability, of necessity.

Something else we've discovered at Makor Or is the necessity of practicing in community. This is how one moves from a sense of oneself as a discrete and separate individual to feeling oneself to be part of something larger. So at Makor Or we insist on daily practice in community. When we are thrown into confrontation with the relentlessness of our dysfunctions, when real transformation beckons and we want to run away, having others present makes it more difficult to do so, partly because we draw strength from them, and partly because we're simply too embarrassed to get up and walk away in the middle of a meditation, the way we might do if we were sitting alone at home.

Disciplined spiritual practice is extremely difficult to sustain, especially when the aforementioned pyrotechnics wear off and we are left with a more acute awareness of our problems than we are comfortable with. Mature practice usually evolves in three stages, but very few practitioners make it out of the second. There is the stage of initial excitement and infatuation, then that passes and there is a long, dry stage often characterized by boredom and frustration. Every spiritual community offers advice as to how to endure this long night of the soul. Some emphasize keeping one's eye on the prize, remembering that boredom and frustration are natural stages on a path that will lead to a great reward: enlightenment, happiness, liberation. Others extol the virtue of boredom and frustration, urging us to develop an appreciation for these states, as one who is accustomed to forests and seascapes might develop an appreciation for the beauty of the desert. After all, boredom and frustration are mind states like any other — like joy, anger, or excitement — with points of interest and worthy features of their own.

Some people are persuaded by these arguments, but very few. What I have found really does keep people around during this long and difficult stage of practice is the sense that they are needed by the community, that if they give up they will be letting their fellows down. It is a fundamental human need to feel needed, to believe that we have a vital and indispensable function to perform in this world on behalf of others. I think we need this even more than we need the gratification that comes from enlightenment or from the apprehension of beauty. Practicing in community keeps us going because we don't want to let the other members of the community down. We feel that they need us, that we are indispensable to them, and this will keep us going for a long time.

But the real value of practicing in community is that it prevents us from having delusions about who we are. We are not discrete egos, hermetically sealed off each from each. We are connected. We are all part of the vast interlinked chain of being, and when we practice together — meditate together, pray together, go through a Sabbath together — this sense of connection becomes very real. We sit together breathing the same air, hearing the same sounds, thinking thoughts in the same almost palpable patterns.

And this deep sense of connection spills over — *cosi revaiyah* — so that when we go out on the street, we can't walk by a homeless person without feeling our connection to them, without acknowledging that their suffering is our suffering, and that we must alleviate it as surely as we would feel that we had to pull out a nail that was stuck in our own leg.

Cal yamei chayai — every day of our lives — we saturate the base of our being, the breath and the body, with awareness. We disarm our unconscious impulses by bringing them into the light, we allow the natural forms and structures of the universe to fill us and to shape our soul, and we allow our suffering to fill us. We open ourselves to God in prayer, and to the profound emptiness at the center of our lives on Shabbat. We enter the interpenetrating flow of being we have always been part of without knowing it. In short, *shavti b'vait Adonai* — we live in the house of Absolute Being, in the House of God, firmly rooted in a place of constant flow, whose momentum sweeps us up in its irresistible thrust until, open-eyed, we fall into heaven.

Acknowledgments

Most of the work in this book was developed over the past thirteen years, first in a series of retreats and workshops on meditation and Jewish practice that I gave together with Zoketsu Norman Fischer, then in the meditation practice I brought into my synagogue, Beth Sholom of San Francisco, and finally at Makor Or, the meditation center adjacent to my synagogue that Norman and I opened together on New Year's Eve, 1999.

Norman and I met on the first day of classes at the Iowa Writers' Workshop in 1968, and we have been extremely close friends ever since. This work arose naturally and directly out of our friendship. He has been a fully equal partner in it and has brought to it a real passion for Judaism, an authentic meditation practice of considerable force, originality both as a teacher and a thinker, and a great heart.

Congregation Beth Sholom of San Francisco showed both

courage and wisdom in supporting this work. Makor Or is, I believe, the only meditation center connected to a synagogue in the world (I really have no way of knowing if this is true or not, but it probably is, and I love to say it anyway), and the leadership of Beth Sholom demonstrated a commendable openness and daring by allowing this work to go forward and then by actively supporting it.

Although in retrospect Makor Or seems to have flowed rather naturally out of the work that Norman and I had been doing for some years, the truth is, it took a real visionary to see where that work was going. That visionary was Rachel Cowan of the Nathan Cummings Foundation. Makor Or was her idea, and grants from the Cummings Foundation carried us through the first four years of our existence. Our debt to both Rachel and to the Cummings Foundation is enormous.

The people of Makor Or, an extraordinary collection of souls, created the practice described in this book by giving their lives to it, by allowing it to touch them deeply and to change them. Neither the practice nor this book would exist without them.

Finally, it must be said that this book was made immeasurably better by the editing of Asya Muchnick and the copyediting of Peggy Leith Anderson, both of Little, Brown and Company. Asya made brilliant revisions and emendations while simultaneously giving birth to a still more brilliant emendation, her daughter, Sabrina Leah. Peg is astoundingly precise with both language and facts, and since I am the kind of person who tends to round reality off to the nearest whole or convenient number, her work on this book was indispensable.

The biblical translations in this book are largely my own, and as close readers will notice, they frequently depart from the King James and other standard versions of the Bible.

About the Author

RABBI ALAN LEW has been the spiritual leader of Congregation Beth Sholom in San Francisco since 1991. Rabbi Lew is the founder and director of Makor Or, the first meditation center connected to a synagogue. He is the author of *One God Clapping: The Spiritual Path of a Zen Rabbi,* numerous works of poetry, and most recently *This Is Real and You Are Completely Unprepared.* Prior to his ordination as a rabbi in 1988 at the Jewish Theological Seminary in New York, he received an MFA from the Iowa Writers' Workshop. Rabbi Lew is married to the novelist Sherril Jaffe.